The Story of G.W. North
A 20th Century Preacher

*From London's East End
to the Warm Heart of Africa*

The Story of G.W. North
A 20th Century Preacher

Judith Raistrick

AMBASSADOR INTERNATIONAL
GREENVILLE, SOUTH CAROLINA & BELFAST, NORTHERN IRELAND

The Story of G.W. North
A 20th Century Preacher

© 2010 Judith Raistrick
All rights reserved

ISBN: 978-1-935507-28-4

Design & Page Layout by Vision

AMBASSADOR INTERNATIONAL
Emerald House
427 Wade Hampton Blvd.
Greenville, SC 29609, USA

AMBASSADOR BOOKS
The Mount
2 Woodstock Link
Belfast, BT6 8DD, Northern Ireland, UK

www.ambassador-international.com

The colophon is a trademark of Ambassador

AUTHOR'S PREFACE

The idea of writing a biography of my father's life has been raised many times. He was asked by some for permission to do so and several people had begun to ask him for material for such an endeavour. No such material having been used, I began to realise that the job was going to be mine. I have been questioned as to whether I was the right person for the task. Someone outside the family may have been able to present a more balanced view of the person and events described in these pages. That granted, I still felt that my father's story was interesting enough to be told and indeed, may prove inspirational to the readers of it. I have also been asked why I am doing this. My reply was that I wanted to help get my father's message out there. I hope I have done this.

If I search my heart as to what my motives have been, I admit that I wanted his grandchildren and great grandchildren as well as the present generation of younger people touched by my father's life to know their heritage and be inspired to follow the examples they have been given, though, as he himself said, 'God hasn't got any grandchildren.'

About a third of the book has been gathered from the subject's own written autobiography, the 'What makes a man tick' address at Auchenheath in 1975 and from information passed on by various members of the family. Some of the story has been pieced together from letters, diaries and articles written for publication. Some of the letters and diaries have never previously been published, so are particularly interesting, especially the ones written from prison.

I am indebted to many friends who have contributed to this narrative both by giving interviews, some of them extensive, and allowing me to use letters and tributes sent in memory of my father. Other people have kindly responded to my request for information for this biography, some of them spending a lot of time putting down their thoughts and memories. Booklets written by Fred Tomlinson; ['Many Learn the Words, Few the Song'] and Jean Boustead: ['A Work of Love'] have been particularly useful.

One purpose of this biography is to try and fit G.W. North into his place in the history of the Charismatic Renewal movement and the history of the House Churches. Norman Meeten states that the Queen's Road Fellowship in Liverpool was the first House Church in this country, beginning in the early 1960s. This book describes how some of these Fellowships came to be formed and the influence they have had in many countries of the world as well as in the U.K.

When I visited Norman, soon after my father's death, to ask him whether he thought a biography should be written, he pointed me to two talks he had recently given on the origins and spread of the Fellowships associated with G.W.North. That was enough to convince me that I should go ahead. I am grateful for his encouragement and for everyone who has urged me on in this somewhat daunting task, including, of course, my husband, who has been endlessly patient and given so much time to the formation of this book that I sometimes think it is as much his work as it is mine.

Andrew Walker, in his book, 'Restoring The Kingdom' [1989] describes G.W. North as 'a truly charismatic figure' whose fellowships 'have their roots before the Charismatic renewal movement'. Peter Hocken, the Catholic writer of 'Streams of Renewal', calls him 'a prominent figure in one of the strands of the House Church movement'. Those who knew him best knew that G.W. always insisted that he never wanted to start a denomination and called Norman Meeten 'The father of the Fellowships.' He has, indeed, been criticised for not having given more thought to organisation. He preferred to leave this to other people, concentrating himself on preaching, writing, teaching and personal work.

Derrick Harrison, himself a Fellowship leader, states in his M.A. thesis [2002]; 'North found himself marginalised, though he was one of the first Charismatics to view Baptism in the Spirit in terms of conversion-initiation.' The thesis examines 'The contribution of G. W. North to the Charismatic Movement in the context of his background influences and his own writings.'

Joyce Thurman's thesis, 'New Wineskins' [1982], includes G. W North in her study of the House Church movement. She describes 'his fellowships' as becoming less important than the other two strands of House Churches which she identifies, perhaps because they were not 'focused on expansion'.

Every effort has been taken to record the facts correctly. Please forgive me if any details are not exactly as you remember them. Most of what has been compiled here is quoted either from what my father himself has said or written or from what my many contributors have said or written. Hopefully this makes for accuracy.

It was sometimes difficult to get the events of the early part of my father's life into the right order. Of course, memories of those times are rather blurred and piecemeal. I hope I have told a coherent story and done justice to the memory of my father, who, as every girl's father should be, was, and is my hero.

Judith Raistrick – January 2010

FOREWORD

This little book has faithfully captured the life and times of an extraordinary man of God and a spiritual father to many believers including myself. It is lovingly written and it breathes the affection that his family and so many of his friends felt for him. There were certain qualities in this man, which made him an inspiring example to those who were privileged to know him. In days of various winds of doctrine and moral decline some will wonder whether a deeper walk with God is at all possible. Is there such a thing as a life of spiritual victory, entering into rest and a deep inner peace with God, overcoming sin and worldliness? Mr. North's life and teaching were testimony to the fact that these things are real and obtainable through simple faith. The hope is that through this biography many more will catch the tone of this man's faith and his walk with God, and enter into the wonderful truth that he discovered. Many of those who knew him will regret that his ministry was not more widely known, for he was truly a prophetic voice.

What then were these qualities that made him such an outstanding man? Humanly speaking, Mr. North was a straightforward man of his word. He was never hypocritical and lived what he believed. Spiritually, he had a raw hunger for God and for holiness. In Bradford God joined him with a people who were thirsting to be led into the deeper things of God. The result was that something happened in that time that marked him out for the rest of his life. He entered into a communion with God in the Holiest place. This was attested to by extraordinary works of power and revelation of the great truths of the New Testament, and in particular of the glory that follows the death and resurrection of Jesus. The great fruit of his long life was that through him God touched so many people, and brought them into a deeper fellowship with God and experience of the cross of Christ through the baptism with the Holy Spirit.

This book had to be written to pass on to others this remarkable testimony. It had to be written so that many more may catch something of the same hunger for God and for holiness and enter into the same life and knowledge of God that was Mr. North's passion and message to his generation.

Les Wheeldon.

INTRODUCTION

'SEE YOU IN THE MORNING!'

Engraved on his headstone near Blantyre in Malawi, these words are remembered by his family as the last words their father said to them before going to bed every night during his latter years.

'We didn't know your Dad was a preacher Marian,' were some of the words written to his daughter, after his funeral on that African hillside. 'You introduced him as Agogo, a Chichewa word meaning Grandfather, but with an Anglicised meaning of a person who is always on the go, so we only knew him as such.'

'No-one wants to hear about me' were the words the preacher had used in Canada just a few years earlier when someone had talked to him about writing his biography. He confessed to having been 'astounded' by this request. 'Such a thing had never crossed my mind,' he said. But he was urged to share his experiences on the grounds that people had read his books and wanted to know about the person behind them and about how his own life had been affected by the things which he had taught. He managed to write 34 pages, but nothing more came of it.

'I certainly didn't want to talk about myself,' were the words he used to explain why he usually refrained from telling stories about his life and ministry during preaching.

'What makes you tick, Mr. North?' was the question put to him at a conference at Auchenheath, Scotland, in 1975. This time he yielded to pressure and related some of his own testimony, hoping to inspire others to prove God's faithfulness. To explain what made him 'tick' he took them right back to his parents and early childhood, emphasising the things which he felt had made him into the preacher that the people had gathered to listen to at the conference. This testimony is available on CD. and on line and is referred to in the following text, together with the autobiographical material started in Canada.

1913, the year when George Walter Govier- North was born, was a difficult year for Britain. It was the year before the outbreak of the First World War, King George V being the reigning monarch. He was the grandson of Queen Victoria, but in London's East End it seems that conditions were reminiscent of some of Charles Dickens' descriptions. The district was well known for poverty and crime. Bethnal Green, where Wally was born in Old Ford Road, is next door to Spitalfields, the then recent haunts of Jack the Ripper, whose notorious deeds still lived on in the memories of Londoners.

So, how did a boy, born to a poor family in the East End of London and destined to end his life in one of the poorest countries in the world, come to preach the Gospel to thousands of people in Britain and abroad? As one writer puts it:

'God used him to bring into being a movement – a movement that has had great influence throughout the world.'

CHAPTER ONE
A PREACHER'S ROOTS

'BLOOD AND FIRE'

Were these stirring words, emblazoned on the Salvation Army flag, prophetic for the baby being dedicated under their banner? Caroline and Walter Govier-North gave their youngest child a great start in life when they took him, carried in the arms of his Uncle Frank, round to Charington Hall. Charington's was a brewery family and the Hall was next door to the brewery. One of the Charingtons had converted to Christ whilst listening to the Salvation Army as they stood playing, singing and preaching in the Mile End Waste, as it was then. Perhaps the smell of the brewery filtering through into the Hall contributed to the fact that the child being dedicated there grew up with an aversion to the kind of beverages being produced.

The baby had weighed in at a bonny, bouncing ten pounds. He himself would remark later, 'I nearly killed my mother when I was born.' He was supposed to have been given the names Walter George, after his father, but his Uncle George had registered the birth and changed the baby's first name to his own, to the displeasure of the parents. He was always called Wally by his family [a rather unfortunate name, as it turned out!]. Maybe it was because of this mix-up that in later years people could never quite work out what to call him.

The house in which the North family lived was shared with a family of Huguenots, of whom Madame Coquille was a lace maker. The Huguenots were descendants of persecuted Protestants from France. They had been stigmatised by the oppressive laws of King Louis 1X and, between 1670 and 1710, had fled to England for refuge in their thousands. They were silk workers and weavers and, after settling in the East End of London, had built their own distinctively styled houses. They were well received in England as sufferers for the Protestant cause, and built many churches, though whether the Coquille family attended a church when the Norths lived there is not clear.

Another large group of people in the East End consisted of a huge number of impoverished East European Jews, who had arrived in London at the end of the 19th century. Pressure had grown on social resources, so much so that one Rabbi had written to his East European counterparts, begging them to warn people in their synagogues not to come to Britain 'on account of poverty and overwork,' saying that it would be 'difficult for them to support themselves and their households.' One of the Jewish boys became Wally's best friend as he grew older.

In this setting of deprivation and over-crowding, Walter and Caroline brought up their family. There had been three other children born to the couple before Wally arrived. Their eldest child, Maud, had been adopted from a Salvation Army Home. Caroline used to foster some of the children from the Home; but Maud was special. She had been the daughter of a friend who had died in childbirth, and this time the arrangement became more permanent.

The other children of the family were Irene [known as Rene], born in 1909 and Francis [known as Frankie], born in 1911. Frankie had apparently been a model child; sweet-tempered and with golden curly hair. Wally recalled that his brother had been held up to him by his mother as an example of good behaviour.

'I didn't have golden hair or nice curls, and I reckon I didn't have a nice curly temper either,' he remembered ruefully, this being a sort of correction.

Tragically, Frankie died from pneumonia at the age of two and a half, following a bout of whooping cough. Wally, though probably now becoming the centre of attention as the only boy and the youngest child, admitted to feeling sad that he had never known his older brother. 'Had he been born today, he would never have died so young,' was Wally's sorrowful observation on his brother's short life. For the first months of his own life he was wheeled around at the bottom of his brother's push chair, never having a pram of his own.

Though Wally himself would have been unaware of them, big sister Rene could remember the London street scenes on which his eyes opened as an infant. She talked of the street criers – 'lavender girls; milk sellers; a knife grinder, using the wheel of his bike to drive the grinder; the rag'n bone man, who gave the children pigs' bladder balloons in exchange for rags; a chair mender, as well as sellers of watercress, shrimps, hot potatoes and chestnuts from a brazier. Barrow boys sold fruit; oranges cost a penny. Milk came in tins; not from cows!'

A railway line; steam trains, of course, ran past the bottom of the garden in Old Ford Road. London traffic at that time consisted of trams, bicycles, a few motor cars and lots of horse-drawn drays. Funeral processions were horse-drawn in the East End, with black plumes on the corners of the carriages and on the horses' heads. Lantern slides at the church were the family's entertainment.

'OPEN THE WINDOWS, CAROLINE'

Wally loved to tell the story of Uncle Frank, his mother Caroline's brother, who died soon after his nephew was born. His mother told him that Uncle Frank used to be 'a terrible man.' One of his many vices was gambling. He was a soldier on the North West Frontier, serving under the British Raj. He 'got saved' in Lucknow, and used to attend meetings at Sandes Soldiers' Home there. One night a preacher stood up at the meeting and declared in the course of his sermon,

'No good ever came from gambling!' At this, Uncle Frank jumped up from his seat and called out,

'Sir, that's not true. I bought this Bible with the last money I ever won at cards!'

"You have to be careful not to make sweeping statements when you're preaching," was the lesson Wally claimed he had learned from this incident.

His mother used to tell him how Uncle Frank would come and stay with her when he came home from India. During this last visit, he would sit in a chair with a cushion on his lap, baby on the cushion, reading from the Bible and praying. Wally liked to think that his uncle had prayed for him to be a preacher, though he didn't remember him at all.

Caroline told her son that, when Uncle Frank lay dying from pneumonia, he had said to her,

'Open the windows, Caroline. I've heard my name called!' She opened the window and he was gone.

Wally later inherited Uncle Frank's Bible. He cherished it, though it was dog-eared, leaves were ripped out and it was written all over – '1912-1913, Lucknow'. It reminded him of 'a Godly, praying Uncle, saved from the depths of sin'. At the Auchenheath conference he gave Uncle Frank as an example of what made him 'tick.' He always felt that he loved Uncle Frank even though he had no memory of him, and placed great value on the prayers of this person whose death had almost coincided with his nephew's birth.

HARD TIMES

Wally also valued the fact that he had himself been taught as a child to pray. 'I learned to pray at my mother's knee. I thank God for it,' was the way he put it. Prayer was to become a great theme of his life and he didn't forget where it all began; with an Uncle who had prayed for him before he could pray for himself.

As a young woman, Wally's mother Caroline had herself become a Christian, resulting in her being kicked out of home by her father. Even though he, as a leather worker, had had the honour of making a handbag for the Tsarina of Russia in the mid eighteen hundreds, he was a 'weekend drunk' and objected to his daughter joining the Salvation Army. After Caroline's mother died he wanted his daughter back at home. He did eventually live with her after she was married to Walter, so she must have forgiven him for his cruel treatment.

Walter Govier-North was not the first young man to whom she had been engaged. But, as she afterwards told her wondering grandchildren, her fiance had 'said something wrong' to her and she had broken off the engagement. They never did find out what he had said!

Walter was a cook when he married Caroline. It was not easy for him to find employment because of his poor eyesight; he was gradually going blind. He worked at various menial jobs, one of them as a window cleaner in the city of London. He also found work as a warehouseman and, latterly, as a bank caretaker. One day, the manager of the bank where he worked was watching him and realised that he could not see. This man kindly told him about a pension for the blind and, to his amazement, he was given new clothes and boots plus a weekly allowance; a little bit of relief in a relentlessly hard landscape.

In common with the other women in the area, work outside the home was a necessity for Caroline. To supplement the family income, early mornings saw her cleaning offices. She did the same again in the evenings, her two young daughters, Maud and Rene, helping her before and after school, emptying waste paper baskets and scrubbing steps along with other jobs. Not much leisure time for them in those difficult days.

Wally was one year old when war broke out in 1914. His father joined the Volunteer Corps to help with the war effort, his eyesight being too poor for him to enlist. Furthermore, he found work as the caretaker of one of the many munitions factories, set up to service the armed forces. Though the work in these places could be extremely dangerous, the North family were glad to be allocated a house near the factory in Lark Lane. After they had moved to this address, Caroline was glad to be given a job with the manager of the factory, tidying his house for him and serving cups of tea to his workers. The war certainly helped the family's employment situation for a time.

Whilst they were living in Lark lane, Wally met a person he later realised had been an early influence in his life. This person was a local Liberal Member of Parliament, named Edwards. He was, according to Wally, 'a good man and a local benefactor'. Besides this, he was a minister at a nearby mission hall where Wally and his sisters were sent to Sunday school every Sunday afternoon.

Wally particularly remembered a special children's anniversary day when he had stood up with the primary class and recited the 'Bible Alphabet'- --A: *A soft answer turneth away wrath.* B: *But foolish words store up anger.* C: *Come unto me.* and so on. In his eighties, Wally confessed to thankfulness in his heart that 'there were those then who cared enough for the souls of girls and boys to give time and patience to teaching little children the Scriptures of truth and imparting to them the knowledge of the Jesus of the Bible.' Indeed, the teaching of those verses must have been remarkably thorough, considering that Wally had been only three or four years old at the time. Good preparation for a preacher? He thought so.

Sadly, after the war, the country staggered from crisis to crisis politically. England 'erupted into class war and the workless poor erupted on to the streets in open rebellion.' Though Wally was too young to be aware of these things, he well remembered a day when he had watched in amazement as mounted police, batons in hand, set their horses' heads into the crowd to disperse the people.

Also sadly, for the North family, there was no more work in munitions after the war and they had to move from Lark Lane to Portman Place, in the same area. They lived here for eight or nine years. It was at that time that Walter had had to take up window cleaning to earn a few pence, though Wally often wondered how 'a man with such poor eyesight could ever hope to see whether a pane of glass was clean.'

He sometimes told the story of how, during this period, his mother was once so desperate for food for her children that she considered going out to steal a loaf of bread. Her Salvation Army convictions told her that what she was contemplating was sinful, but her children were crying out for food. She had prayed, but there had been no answer. What turmoil must have filled her mind!

Just as she had been about to go out to do the unthinkable, a knock came at the door. It was Mrs. Cave, a friend from the church, with a loaf in her hand. God had provided; but, 'Who would have blamed her?' said Wally of his mother's intentions. It must have pained him to think of her in such a state of need. Obviously times were hard and the children grew up often in want of the necessities of life.

'We were, as a family, greatly disadvantaged,' was Wally's summary of his early childhood. But, on the contrary, he considered it really to have been an advantage to him. Was not Jesus born into a poor family, and did He not say that He had been sent to preach the Gospel to the poor?

BIG, SILVER CIGARS

This was how Wally described the Zeppelins which flew over London during the First World War. He had a recollection of seeing them on his way home from the hospital, where he had been recovering from diphtheria. But a more vivid memory was of the 'loathsome' boiled rice on which the patients were fed. He never did take kindly to eating rice after that.

The Zeppelins were airships, used for scheduled flights before World War One. People had only just got used to the idea of passenger flights when war broke out and the Germans began to use the Zeppelins on bombing and scouting missions. Little wonder that they became known as 'baby-killers'. As he sat and watched them during air-raids young Walter would wonder why everyone was running, not feeling the fear felt by the adults. Remarkably perhaps, none of the family was hurt during these incidents. They always knew when a raid was coming when they heard a knock on the door to rouse Father. They had to open their doors, front and back, to let people run through to shelter under the arches of the railway viaduct behind their house. Big sister Rene recalls,

'We ran in the opposite direction from all the others and the police would try to stop us. We ran to the house of Mr and Mrs Cave, a dear old Methodist couple. He was a carver and guilder of picture frames. We all went down into the cellar for safety. We sang hymns and laughed and joked during the air raid, but were hushed up if there was a loud bang, so people could hear what was falling. I remember seeing a Zeppelin alight in the sky, like a huge flaming cigar, and people cheering and clapping as it came down.

We were never really afraid during air-raids - our Dad was on duty [as a Volunteer] - and Mum would comfort us with assurances of God's love and care for us. It was quite exciting for us children; getting up at night; putting on overcoats and running to the Caves', where there'd be a big enamel pot, full of scalding hot tea - quite an adventure! It felt lovely running home to bed after a raid and getting a biscuit as a treat.'

When the sirens sounded Wally would be picked up out of bed, wrapped in a blanket, put into a pushchair and wheeled off. During one of these raids his aunt, whose husband was away in the army, was pushing him down to the Cave's house. Crowds of people were rushing the other way, and some of them shouted to Aunt Edie,

'You're going the wrong way!' He recalled looking up into his Aunt's face and saying,

'God won't let them hurt us, Auntie, will He?'

So the children were brought up to have confidence in God's care for them, and indeed, the house of Mr and Mrs Cave provided a refuge for local Christians. Wally could dimly recall being laid on a bed of straw which was spread out on the cellar floor and staring at all the people. One face which particularly fascinated him was the pockmarked face of a blind man called Uncle Charley, who played the accordion and led the hymn-singing with a powerful musical voice. So, though these were terrible days for this country, Wally could only remember them as 'unforgettable; a joyous memory'.

He pointed out that, though their doors were left wide open at these times for many hours and many people passed through the house, nothing was stolen or broken. 'We were fleeing from a common enemy,' he said, 'and, in any case, there was nothing much to take. We were all poor. Is anything much else to be gained by war than death and destruction?'

At last came the most outstanding day in the young boy's mind; Armistice Day, 11th November 1918, when an agreement was signed between the Germans and the Allied armies to end the war. Wally remembered that,

'The streets of London became banqueting halls and the night became bright with bonfires and fireworks. Pavements were full of tables and chairs and every household that could do so contributed to the feast. Singing and dancing replaced fears and miseries in the streets. It was transfixing to me.' He emphasised that that was 'the real Armistice Day. Nothing was organised. There were no artificial poppies; no Cenotaph or massed bands; it was real. There can never be another one like that one.'

How wonderful it must have been when, after the war, there was some alleviation of the daily grind of London. In the summer, if there was any work available, the whole family, along with crowds of other East Enders, would travel down to the Kent countryside for the hop picking and fruit picking. It was like a summer holiday for them and their only means of leaving the East End streets.

The excitement of the children knew no bounds as they moved into huts with corrugated iron roofs on Old Soar Farm. What freedom they found picking hazelnuts in the hedgerows. But they had to help with the hop picking and catch rabbits for the pot when the corn was harvested. Of course, no work was allowed on Sundays; instead they walked to Sunday school at the local church.

Another happy memory for Wally was the sound of his mother's singing.

'God had blessed my mother with a wonderful voice,' he said. He was often woken by the sound of her singing and playing on the harmonium, practising for her solo spots on the streets with the Salvation Army. In those days they went every Sunday to Clapham Junction, where the trains would be halted from 11am until midday. Every train, by law, had to pull into a station during the hour of morning worship.

'The call to worship and the hearing of God's word sometimes failed to attract people from their comfortable carriages, but when Mother began to sing her solos, accompanying herself on the harmonium, the trains soon began to empty,' was the story. And when she sang in any open-air meetings, the police would have to move people on to stop the listening crowds from holding up the traffic. Wally would often tell his children about his mother's 'wonderful voice'. He wished they could have heard her in her younger days when Gran's voice had been at its strongest. It had certainly made an impression on him!

SIGNING THE PLEDGE

'One of the foundational things on which my life has been built was laid in my heart in those years, never to be removed,' remembered Wally. 'One of these was a strong dislike for the drinking of alcohol. When I saw men lying on the pavement drunk, and heard the mumbling speech of the old ladies, and smelt the stink through the open doors of pubs in summer time, dislike and hatred of drink and tobacco smoke filled my heart.'

After the war, vivid memories of the family who had lived in the house opposite theirs in Portman Place were enough to fill the young boy's heart with fear. The father of this large family was a big man and his son was bigger still and a boxer. One night the North family was woken by a thumping on their door and a huge row going on across the street. All the family from over the road streamed in through their open door, crying and screaming. The children were frightened because the son had broken a large vase over the father's head.

Incidents such as these, common in the East End, made him think, 'So that is what drink does!'

To try to counteract the effects of drink, the Methodist church at the top of their street ran a Tuesday night Band of Hope meeting for children, Wally and his sisters among them. It was packed with hundreds of youngsters for the Magic Lantern shows which were always directed against the drinking of alcohol. Without fail, each of these shows finished with the screening of The Pledge, which everyone recited together:

'I promise, by God's help to abstain from all intoxicating liquors as beverages.'
Wally could still repeat that pledge into his eighties.

'I wonder how many have kept that promise,' he would ask, 'But I meant it, and have kept that promise I made to Him in Gordon Hall so long ago.' His sisters have also kept that promise, so great was the impression made by those meetings and the scenes which inspired them. He has since reflected that it would probably be frowned upon in these days to coerce children into making such promises, and that even Christians would say that it would not be wrong to break any such commitments. He would beg to differ!

Wally has described how his Christian upbringing, as well as keeping him from alcohol, stopped him joining in with the rest of the boys in the street in their unclean jokes, swearing, vulgarity, gambling and card games. He restricted himself to Cowboys and Indians, football, cricket, marbles, hopscotch and climbing lamp posts. He knew how to play cards by watching the other boys, but something stopped him from doing it himself. He didn't remember having been being persecuted for this behaviour; everyone in the street knew that a Christian family wouldn't approve of gambling games.

ITCHY PARK

After the move to Portman Place, their last London address, the family association with the Salvation Army came to an end. Caroline maintained that she had not been pleased when the Salvation Army began to collect money during their open-air meetings, though this may not have been the whole story. Whatever the reason, they all began to attend the nearby Methodist Church on Sunday mornings. Wally sat with his sisters and regularly went to sleep. There were no morning Sunday schools in those days; but the children were sent to Sunday school in the afternoon.

Having ceased their activities with the Salvation Army, Walter and Caroline now began to work with a group of people of no particular denominational ties, drawn together by a common desire to help the down and outs. They called themselves The Christian Community, meeting in a hall in Whitechapel. All their activities were directed towards 'the salvation of the destitute, the poor and the unwanted'. As an infant Wally was taken every week by his mother to this hall, where she would help distribute hunks of new bread along with tin mugs of cocoa or coffee to the homeless street people. He never forgot that dingy room, filled with the smell of delicious food and drink.

Soon after the food was given out singing commenced. In Wally's own words:

'My mother would sit at the rather large harmonium and play and sing to these poor, underfed, under clothed, unclean people, who, at times, in between mouthfuls of bread and cocoa, would sing with her a half-remembered verse of a hymn. I can never forget one of these afternoons; I was sitting on the front row of chairs near to my mother, when she called me to her, so I went. Picking me up, she stood me on top of the instrument and announced that I was about to sing to them all. She played a chord with which I was very familiar. The words of the chorus went:

> O, come, come to Jesus, Come, come to Jesus, Come, come to Jesus,
>
> And He will take you in.
>
> And if you're discontented and weary with your sin,
>
> Come, come to Jesus and He will take you in.'

Wally must have been 3 or 4 years old when this happened, but it had obviously imprinted itself on his mind. The people loved his solo. It was to be the first of many, for he developed a beautiful singing voice. This introduction was to set the tone for the next ten years of his life, and indeed, for a lifetime of public service.

Wally was only about eight years old when his father decided that he was old enough to begin to join the adults of the Christian Community on their visits to the notorious lodging houses of Whitechapel. On Sunday evenings the family would split up. Caroline would take the girls with her to Mildmay Mission Hospital, where the matron used to conduct a service for the patients. This hospital, which had its origins in the cholera outbreak of 1866, has always stressed its role as a Christian centre as well as a hospital. Walter would take his son with him to join a band of workers preaching the Gospel to the homeless.

The walk to Whitechapel was a long one and lay through the erstwhile haunts of Jack the Ripper. This area has been described by some late nineteenth century commentators as being, 'the worst criminal rookery of London', and Flower and Dean Street, where the Christian workers met, as being, 'perhaps the foulest and most dangerous street in the metropolis'. In 1903 social commentator, Jack London, highlighted 'Itchy Park' in Spitalfields, as 'a notorious rendezvous for homeless vagrants'.

Not a place for children, it could be said.

Everyone being gathered in Flower and Dean Street, the workers spent a few minutes in prayer, before splitting into small groups. That was Wally's cue for getting behind the harmonium, mounted on pram wheels. He was delighted to be allowed to push it along the streets of Spitalfields to the lodging houses. It cost the lodgers only a few pence per night for a place in one of these wretched shelters; but sometimes they could not even afford that. It was not uncommon 'to find against some wall in a corner, what appeared to be a heap of newspapers or sacking which turned out to be a human being'..

'Inquisitive, I looked and wondered, cold enough myself in the freezing winds; but I was too young and too helpless to understand or do anything,' remembered Wally. It was scenes such as these which reinforced the repeating of the Pledge.

'I have thanked God that He kept me from such bondage,' he once wrote.

Describing the scene in one of the lodging houses, as he could remember it, Wally related:

'I've gone in when you couldn't see across the room, where they were cooking on a great communal fire. The place was filled with tobacco smoke from numerous pipes. The fug was tremendous. Somebody was frying kippers; somebody was roasting sausages and somebody was boiling tea. Cockroaches, it seemed to me in hordes, ran up the walls and over the tables, and men, uncouth and unkempt, stood or sat and smoked and spat, or cooked and talked, ate and drank, or put snuff up their noses.

Where they all slept I had no idea, until one day I was told that they slept on a clothes line. It was fastened on a hook or staple in the wall and stretched across the room to another one on the opposite wall. The men then sat on the floor, alternately facing the front or rear of the room, leaned their backs on the rope and slept. I was amazed and incredulous and thought how blest I was to have such a good father and mother, a nice home and a good bed to sleep in.

Looking back, as I often have done, on those days, I think the most outstanding thing to me is the fact that my father and mother allowed me to sit with a man who always wanted me to sit on a bench at the front of the meeting. He was always drunk and maudlin, dirty and unshaven and he used to put his arm around me, hugging me close, drooling over me, and with his free hand he constantly put pinches of snuff up his nose, with the result that he was constantly sneezing. I thought he was abominable!

I was the proud owner of a watch, which I kept in my top pocket. I used to guard my watch as I believed everybody was a rogue in the lodging house. One thing the war did was blow these places to bits around Bethnal Green and the East End. They've had to rebuild. It's an ill wind that blows nobody any good. I honour my parents and those like them, who *Out of their poverty, made many rich*, and mixed with and ministered to those who, worse off than themselves, sought to keep body and soul together, living communally in dimly lit kitchens that all decent people avoided. How good God was to me that in my early days I was allowed to mix with the poor and the outcasts of society; with the drunks and the lawbreakers and those who had given up all hope of human dignity; those who begged and stole in order to prolong a life not worth living and to wonder if God had forgotten them, perhaps.'

While the party led by Wally's father was in the men's house, another party would be in the women's house, a few streets away. Later these two parties joined together for a third meeting in yet another house. One thing Wally remembered about this third house was the large square carpet on which they had stood. He recalled:

'I thought this indicated that this house was a bit above the one we had just left, but my illusion was swiftly dispelled when I heard the real purpose of the carpet. It was placed there, or so I was informed, to hide a large trap door through which unsuspecting persons were let down into an underground cellar where they were robbed of everything of value.'

Sometimes Wally's mother and sisters joined them for the last session. He could always remember the wonderful music when the rich bass voice of one of the lodgers, a West Indian man, joined those of his mother and father in the singing. Sister Rene recalls that in the lodging houses, 'Maud would play the harmonium and Wally would sing to the homeless men. He would have been about eight years old and had a beautiful voice. Then a tram ride home – a penny for an adult and ha'penny for a child. What a treat!'

Wally's mother would sometimes take in lodging house people.

'One night she brought a woman home,' he remembered, 'and slept in bed with her, father vacating his bed for the night. Mother woke up lousy in the morning. That's the kind of way I was brought up. We used to get down in the filth - beds were shared.' Wally would sometimes suffer at school when nits and fleas were found on him, but, 'That's how I began,' he said. 'I liked it.'

So, the idea of working for and preaching the Gospel to the local population was well and truly worked into Wally in his early years. He considered it a wonderful start in life, and to have played a big part in what made him 'tick'.

HARD WORK NEVER KILLED ANYBODY

Wally could remember walking to school with his sisters as an infant. He could recall sitting by the coke stove which burned in the classroom. Maybe, as was sometimes the case at that time amongst the poorer classes of society, and as Wally himself afterwards wondered, he would have been sent to school with his older siblings before he was of school age so that his mother could go to work.

Wally was often plagued by 'bilious attacks' as a child and he was suffering from one of these when the time came for him to sit the exam for the grammar school. Because of this he could not complete the question paper. Even though the questions he had managed to answer were correct, no second chance was given. So he missed out on his opportunity for a higher education; but never considered this to have been unfortunate.

Perhaps as a result of these attacks of nausea, Wally attended the local Portman Place School at the start of his secondary education. But he was 'a little above' the other pupils, for he soon left it and was sent to a Central School. The London County Council Education Committee's handbook for Elementary Schools for 1911 states that, 'The chief object of the Central School is to prepare girls and boys for immediate employment on leaving school.' The aim was that the trend of the education should be 'eminently practical'. The education provided was definitely of a higher grade than that of ordinary secondary schools.

'I believe I was a cut above Portman and a cut below Grammar,' Wally reflected. 'Education has not become a Sacred Cow in our family; we were definitely working class and, very nearly as a tenet of belief, I grew up to accept the axiom, *Hard work never killed anybody* as almost a proverb. The dictum of the Apostle Paul was held tenaciously by our family; *If a man will not work, neither shall he eat*. But my education amongst the poor and needy of Whitechapel proceeded weekly, as I was taken there Sunday after Sunday by my father.'

Perhaps his schooling would have proceeded to a higher standard if he had remained in London, but it turned out that he attended the Central School for only two years. However, it seems clear that his family's attitude towards schooling contributed to his on-going somewhat dismissive attitude towards higher education. He feared that it was the downfall of many, and not necessary [as he proved] for the work of God. It was not part of what made him 'tick', though one of his colleagues in the Fellowships described him as being 'a man of considerable intellect, although he used to say he had no education. He had a mind like a steel trap. He was very, very bright.'

As for Christian doctrine, the family, though loosely connected with Methodism, does not seem to have been strongly convinced of any particular aspect of teaching, though Wally distinctly remembered his mother's tone when she said,

'Mr. Y. does not believe in Hell!' From this he concluded that his parents were not entirely satisfied with the preaching at the Methodist Church they attended and of which at one time they had been caretakers. He could not recall being taught any of the great Christian doctrines, but was left to develop freely, 'For which,' he said, 'I am grateful.'

WHAT'S IN A NAME?

The name of Govier-North was considered a nuisance by the all members of the family, and they were always known as the Norths; but the way in which Wally acquired this name could be one of the reasons for his teetotalism. He told the story himself:

'My father's brother John was a successful business man of some wealth; married, but childless. One evening he was in the West End of London and, to his amazement and anger, he saw his wife standing in a theatre queue with another man. This, apparently, was the cause of separation. My Uncle left wife, home and country for Quebec in Canada, where he changed his name from North to Govier and set up in business again.

Being childless, he asked my father if he would adopt his new name, hyphenating it with his own. For this he would be granted a certain sum of money. He agreed to do this. Somehow my grandmother and an aunt were included in the arrangement, and both, I believe, were addicted to drinking. The result of all this was that, by the time I was born, the money was gone, but the surname was not!'

What Wally does not mention here is that Govier, the name chosen by his uncle, was an old family name. It was recorded in the Parish Register of Ilminster in March 1815 that Elizabeth, daughter of Robert Govier, Guard of Coach, and Hannah, was married to Charles North, Veterinary Surgeon. It seems that the fortunes of the family fluctuated, but the name stuck. Perhaps it is just as well that the name has now died out!

Biographer's note:- As we have seen, there was confusion about Wally's name right from the beginning of his life, and, in later years, he became known by various appellations. He was addressed as Pastor, of course, by the people of Bradford and Loose and usually as Mr. North by the people he met after this, though a few, generally older people, called him Wally or George. When referred to in his absence, he was often called GW. [George Walter], hence the wide use of those initials in this book. If this seems confusing it is because that is how it was!

His colleague, Norman Meeten, when asked, for this biography, why he thought GW. was not usually called by his Christian name, replied,

'He never gave us permission.' This is undoubtedly true, and has been referred to in 'Many learn the words, few the song' by Fred Tomlinson. He says there that,

'The issue of how Mr. North was or should be addressed was an issue which never quite went away. His position on the subject was, what we may call, old school. He believed it proper, particularly for younger people, to show respect by using the term 'Mr.' Fred describes how GW. castigated his old friend, Dave Wetherly, for allowing young people to call him Dave; but 'Dave could never bring himself to request the change.'

G.W., however, showed that he didn't take the issue too seriously when, in the U.S., he met a young man, who welcomed him with the words,

'Hi, I'm Willy!'

'Hi, I'm Wally!'

   G.W. was of an older generation than those he came to work with and, as Norman said, he never did ask people to call him by his Christian name [or names!]. But some of them referred to him as The White-haired Gentleman or even The Boss or The General. More irreverent titles, if used, are unknown to the author!

Plaxtol school 1926
Wally 7th from left back row, Dolly - seated - 2nd from right, middle row

18th Birthday

CHAPTER 2
A PREACHER IS FORMED

A COUNTRY BOY

A great transformation took place in the lives of the North family when, in 1926, they moved from Bethnal Green to the Kent countryside. Their daughter Maud had been in fragile health and it was because of this that they left the streets of London for the small village of Plaxtol. The contrast couldn't have been greater. There were now no more pea-souper fogs, caused by London 'smog', to face every winter. Wally remembered that, as well as Maud's, 'The health of the whole family improved greatly. The removal was life-changing. The rush of life ceased.' Having himself survived pneumonia as well as diphtheria and also escaped uninjured after falling from a bedroom window, he had good reason to think that God had preserved his life.

When he first set eyes on his new home Wally was incredulous.

'There was not another house in sight!' was his happy impression of that day. He could hardly believe what he was seeing. A large white house with a pink tiled roof stood alone in about an acre of ground not far from the village. It was called Cage House. He could never have imagined being able to live in a place like this. The house was rented by Wally's father from the owner of Old Soar Farm, where the family had worked during previous summers. Excitement and relief at being away from the crowded East End filled all their hearts. Sevenoaks, the nearest town, was seven miles away.

No time was lost in making good use of Cage House, part of the grounds speedily being turned into a hen run. Running the length of the hedge bordering the road was a row of apple trees. A decorative beech hedge conveniently divided the garden into two; a flower garden and a vegetable garden.

The garden looked 'enormous' to the eyes of a London boy who knew nothing of gardening and the fact that Wally was the one who had to look after it tended to outweigh the advantages in his eyes. On top of that, he was dismayed to discover that the house was not on mains water and that all water had to be pumped into a storage tank in the loft by a pump which was fifty yards from the house. He was immensely relieved to find that the pump was motorised and that all he had to do was to look after the engine. 'If that broke down,' he said, 'I had to carry the water up to the house in buckets, climb up a ladder to the loft and pour water into the tank. Life in the country was not all I had imagined it to be!

But I soon learned to be a country boy, and gardening, pumping water and chopping up firewood soon ceased to be threats and became a way of life. All these were after school activities and, as we never had any homework, there was always plenty of time for them. *Satan findeth mischief for idle hands to do* soon found its way into my mind from my mother's lips, and we all believed it. Playing in the street was a thing of the past and acquainting myself with grass and hedgerows and the creatures that lived in them took its place. Children born and bred in towns miss so much.'

If all this sounds like rather heavy work for a young boy, it was probably because his father was still working in London, some thirty miles away, that Wally often had to be the man of the house. Life was tough too for his sisters, Maud and Rene, who had left school by this time. Mr. Little, the owner of Cage House, also owned a number of farms. He set the girls to work doing whatever seasonal jobs were available. Rene remembered her frozen fingers, caused by picking Brussels sprouts 'with ice on them in the winter'. The girls also had to pile up potatoes in heaps and cover them with straw, leaving a ventilation hole at the top.

In spite of these hardships, according to Rene, the food was much better in Kent than in London:

'In the garden were pear, plum and apple trees. Mum made lots of jam and stewed fruit - delicious on cornflakes for breakfast or on porridge in winter. We grew our own vegetables and flowers. Eggs could be bought from the farm; and milk in a tin with a lid and a handle. Bread came hot from the local bakery. We had fresh meat twice a week.'

Her father was doing a cleaning job at that time, though he had very limited vision and now wore thick glasses. She said that 'he couldn't resist a bargain, sometimes to the cost of the family, who struggled to keep fed and clothed. Finally, when he was registered as fully blind, he had to give up work.'

The girls were able to leave the farm when a woman co-worker found them jobs at Roughway Paper Mill. There the work consisted of sorting rags for paper-making. After removing buttons and elastic they had to slice the rags into strips on blades protruding from the bench. It seems Health and Safety was not around then!

WALLY MEETS DOLLY

Meanwhile, Wally, aged thirteen at the time of the move from London, was attending the village school. It was there that he first met a local girl in the year below him, named Dorothy [Dolly] Coppins. She was born in Dunks Green, a hamlet near Plaxtol, and was the second oldest child in an expanding family which eventually comprised eight children. Her parents were named Mary and Joseph, so perhaps she had to be special!

Dolly's older sister Nell recalls that Dolly was 'very bright at school, much brighter than I was. She could sing and join in anything at the school or at the chapel.' She must have been a good actress because she starred as Britannia in a school drama. Her co-star was Wally North as John Bull in this patriotic Empire Day production. It was a date which would later become much more significant in the actors' lives, being the date on which they were to marry in 1941. It does not seem to have been love at first sight, though, as Dolly thought her future husband was a 'Big head!' In their final years Dolly was made head girl and Wally head boy of Plaxtol School, so they must both have been outstanding pupils.

Wally did not attend the school for long, the school leaving age in those days being fourteen, but whilst there he excelled at sport. He was made 'captain of the cricket team, played right wing at football, ran a leg in the 220, was champion shot putter and champion weight lifter in the team that took the cup at the Kent County Schools Athletic Championship at Sevenoaks.'

'O, for the wings of a dove' was one of his solos as lead singer in the school choir. When she had first heard him sing, his surprised teacher had asked,

'Wherever did you get that voice?'

She herself had been a singer, training with famous performers of the day, but had had to give up her career and take up school teaching when something had happened to her throat. She gave Wally singing lessons and wanted him to have his voice trained. His beautiful treble singing voice gradually descended to a tenor and remained strong into old age; but his singing career at the time was confined to solos at school concerts and at the chapel. Besides, his parents could never have afforded singing lessons.

Being musically versatile, he also learned to play the violin at school. He must have been fairly good at this to play duets, as he did, with his music teacher. He gained two Royal Academy certificates. Whenever, in future years, he was asked why he had not taken up music or singing as a career his reply was,

'I didn't want to. I always considered them to be Bypath Meadows.' But maybe, at that early stage, God had used the limited means of his parents to steer Wally's life on a different path in his personal 'Pilgrim's Progress'. His violin was put away for many years, but when his daughters were teenagers they would sometimes urge Dad to play them a tune on it, and, with protestations of not being any good, he would oblige, showing them that he had been too modest about his abilities.

KEEPING THE PLEDGE

Wally did not have many jobs open to him when he left school. Farming, papermaking and private [domestic] service were the three major sources of employment for school leavers in the district.

'I was speedily set to work,' said Wally. 'Generally in those days children were allowed little or no choice in job selection, so when I was told that a position had been chosen for me I went to it. My parents had found for me a place in private service at Old Alleyns, so, without demur, I was installed in the house of an architect where I functioned as houseboy. I earned 10 shillings a week. Learning that I could earn more money at Roughway Paper Mill, I sought and found work there for the sum of 15 shillings a week. I worked 45 hours a week and from there I was offered a job as beaterman's assistant at 30 shillings a week, doing 12 hour day and night shifts, totalling 60 hours a week. It was hard work, but I had often heard it said that hard work never killed anyone, and I proved it to be so.' [A beaterman's work was to mix scrap paper with hot water and chemicals to make pulp for new paper].

In his spare time, as well as playing football for the firm on Saturday afternoons, Wally still had a big vegetable and flower garden to attend to. He did not mention in his hand-written story that in their leisure time he and his friends got up to some fairly dare-devil activities, one of which was fulfilling a dare to walk around the top of the mill chimney!

During Wally's years of employment the paper mill grew in prosperity. He relates the story of the expansion of the building:-

'We all watched and waited patiently for the completion of the work and the grand opening ceremony which was to take place. When that great day arrived the mill was brought to a standstill and silence and we were all gathered in the new building to hear the speeches and to drink health and prosperity to all. At the appropriate time men came round with bottles of wine and other strong drink so that we could all toast the mill. When they came with the drinks to me I politely refused strong drink and asked if I could have lemonade. This produced, I joined in the toast. That pledge, so regularly made every Tuesday evening, some twenty years earlier, was still holding fast; it had been so real.

I tell this story because a woman who worshipped at our chapel had been watching me throughout the whole ceremony to see what I would do when the drinks came round. This was unknown to me, but on the following Sunday she told me that when she saw how I refused strong drink she plucked up courage to refuse it also. It is not an easy thing to stand amongst workmates and keep a promise made to God.'

The emphasis was not on the evils of alcohol, but on the importance of keeping one's vows.

EDWIN TAYLOR

The North family, as they had in London, began their life in Plaxtol by attending a Methodist Church. Walter and Caroline, however, could find no satisfaction there, so they left the church and sought elsewhere. The last straw had been hearing the superintendent speak on 'Why I am a modernist'.

They found that there was a Congregational church in the neighbouring hamlet of Dunks Green and began to attend the services there. They discovered that, whilst the building was owned by the Congregationalists, the people were led by Mr. Edwin Taylor, a man of Brethren background.

He had been a Conscientious Objector during the Great War. Before his C.O. tribunal he had been a successful commercial artist in London, working as manager of Fleet Street Studios.

Following the tribunal, Mr. Taylor had moved to the countryside and found himself a job as a milkman. Seeing the chapel standing empty and unused, he requested the use of it and set about the evangelisation of the village, preaching in the building and in the open air. Here he became the target of much barracking and many missiles. In Wally's words:

'He was an avowed Protestant and made sure everyone knew it. He firmly opposed Father Philips, who presided over the High Church in Plaxtol. This prelate loved whisky and practised many Romish ways. He placed a crucifix in the church grounds and, when he died, was buried under it. He spoke of God as being the clerk of the weather. I needed little more disrespectful evidence than that to convince me that he did not know God.'

Wally describes how Mr. Taylor 'used his art, as well as his mouth, for the spread of the Gospel.' He was to inherit some of Mr. Taylor's pictures and he often used them himself when giving talks to children. The family particularly remember a large picture, which was really a working model of Noah's Ark, fascinating to the children. Another outstanding one which Wally often used was a reproduction of Holman Hunt's 'Light of The World'. On the back of this picture Mr. Taylor had painted weeds all around the door. He had added three bolts with three things written on them which would keep Jesus out. These could be drawn back to let Him in. It was a powerful tool for evangelism to both adults and children.

Wally thought that Edwin Taylor was 'one of the most brave and courageous men' he had ever met, and that his wife was 'one of the sweetest and gentlest women'. He went on, 'He was such a great man and I owe so much to him. He had been a redhead and the fiery nature which is said to accompany such hair had not left him. He was every inch a fighter, as devoted to his wife as to God. They had the reputation among the villagers of being lovebirds, which is about the highest compliment that can be paid to any married couple.'

Wally was impressed by the fact that the Taylors headed their notepaper with a quotation from the epistle of Jude - *Earnestly contending for the faith which was once delivered unto the saints*. 'And they did just that,' he said. 'I am thankful that they also taught me to do just that. It was a brave person who stood up to him.'

Edwin Taylor, it seems, became an important figure in the area, and was a man much admired for all he did for the neighbourhood. The estate manager of a local millionaire said that he, Mr. Taylor, had 'changed the inhabitants of Dunks Green from being a bunch of thieves into decent people.' So perhaps the standard of behaviour had not been much better in the country than it had in London.

After the War, Mr. Taylor went back to work in London. 'How he managed to accomplish all he did was of no small wonder to me,' Wally declared, 'for, though he lived and laboured among us, he worked in London, travelling up to the city every day.'

At the chapel, he sought to teach the young people, in Wally's words, 'separation from the world, as well as salvation from sin - *being in the world but not of it*. He took this youth from London and moulded me, training me to teach, preach and, most important of all, to know the Bible.' Indeed, the desire to study the Bible must have been strongly implanted in Wally's young mind at this time. He would buy bags of sweets and, instead of reading novels, would read his Bible whilst eating them!

The North family became committed to Mr. Taylor's ministry and, although Wally eventually parted company with Edwin Taylor, he always honoured his memory and paid tribute to the great influence his old pastor had had on his life. He included the story of Mr. Taylor in his explanation of what made him 'tick'.

'I thank God for him,' Wally said. 'They [the Brethren] more or less taught me The Book from cover to cover. It stands me in good stead.' Under this 'devoted' ministry, Wally became familiar with the Scriptures. Having aptitude and natural gifts, he was promoted, as he grew up, to various church activities and offices. He came top in every Bible Exam; in due time becoming youth leader, Sunday school superintendent, treasurer, secretary and deacon. Aged 18, he went through Believer's Baptism.

Mr. Taylor started a Young Peoples' Fellowship at which he taught the youth of his flock to chair meetings and pray in public. He would set subjects for them to preach on, gently criticising their presentation, their manner and their material.

'He never criticised prayer,' Wally remembered. 'He said God hears you, even if you speak backwards.'

Wally's spiritual education during this period was furthered by attending Brethren conferences to hear distinguished preachers and teachers. He rapidly developed an ability to preach himself, Mr. Taylor encouraging and training him to be a speaker, both in the chapel and in the open air, as often as three times a week during the summer. He seemed to have it all, being musically gifted and able to preach. Visiting dark country pubs to give out tracts was the norm for him. He described himself as being, 'a believer, a leader and a teacher,' but, he added, 'I was not born again. I was never, that I can remember, ever pointedly asked if I was saved.' What would his answer have been to such a question?

At the Auchenheath conference, G.W. wanted to emphasize that it was because of his natural abilities that he had been accepted as a Christian worker.

'I'd always been a believer; I'd always prayed,' he said.

In his hand written account he stated,

'I discovered later, though I didn't know it then, that one of the greatest tragedies of the Church these days is that they too often mistake natural talent for spiritual gift.'

He could not remember being taught any specific doctrines or dogmatic theology. He did not know at the time that Mr. Taylor was a convinced Calvinist, had once been a lecturer in a Calvinist College and had written a book on Calvinist Doctrine. Indeed, he didn't know that Calvinism and Arminianism existed and were great bones of contention in the evangelical world.

Though, with hindsight, G.W. realised some of the shortcomings of his spiritual upbringing, at the time he flourished under Mr. Taylor's ministry and always paid tribute to the foundational teaching and example of his old pastor.

'I loved it all,' he said, 'and when he approached me one day with the suggestion that he would like to put my name forward to some of his friends that I should go to their churches and preach, it was as wonderful as it was unexpected. Yet not *so* unexpected, as I had known for some time that I would be a preacher of the Gospel. I always wanted to be.'

HOW DID YOU LEARN TO PREACH LIKE THAT?

Edmund Clark, one of the visiting speakers at the chapel, was a man who had given his life to youth work. He was the organiser of a boys' camp which used to pitch on Camber Sands, a lovely flat stretch of sand on the East Coast.

'The campers were a strange mix,' wrote Wally, 'hailing from varsity men down through public and private school boys to a mixture of missionaries' children and elementary school boys, of whom I had been one. The first year I went to camp as one of the boys and in succeeding years as a tent leader.' One particular evening at the camp stood out in Wally's mind:

'Following the evening meal we stayed in the large marquee singing hymns till the message was delivered. Being a tent leader, I was asked to give the message one night. I therefore stood before the assembled company of my peers and gave the message. I do not remember what I preached on; but I, late of Bethnal Green, and now a country boy, was addressing varsity men, missionaries and preachers of some reputation!

Some time later, a group of undergraduates and graduates were out for a walk and I was among them. Amongst other questions I was asked –

"Where and how did you learn to preach like that?"

"The time you gave to your books, studying to get your degrees, I gave to the Bible."

They were a lovely group of young men; all brought to silence. I wondered at my temerity.'

When telling this story at Auchenheath, G.W. paused to reflect: *'Whatsoever a man soweth, that shall he also reap* is a statement none can deny. Life is for investment. In the sight of God careers can be little more than the waste of a life and ambition a drive to everlasting death.' He added that he had related this event in the hope that it would be of value to others. Knowledge of the Bible and the God of the Bible, as opposed to the knowledge education can give, were repeatedly stressed throughout his ministry.

GW. emphasized that Mr Taylor's input into his life was a huge part of what made him 'tick.' But one particular event in which Edwin Taylor and his congregation took part was to have a truly life changing effect on the young preacher and result in disagreement with his pastor.

DOLLY'S STORY

Dolly began to go to Sunday school at the age of three and, even at that young age, remembered having a desire to follow God. Her father, though often the worse for drink, encouraged his children to pray and go to Sunday School. He was a man much loved by his neighbours for his medical skills, learned in the army medical corps in World War One. These skills were greatly valued in the village community, especially as he would never worry about payment for his readily given services. But no provision had been made for soldiers returning home after the carnage of the First World War. So times were particularly hard for this family as well as for many others.

Dolly and her older sister Nell were both sent into jobs in domestic service after leaving school at the age of fourteen. Dolly made her response to the Lord at the age of sixteen. Her friend Olive recalls that, 'Mr. Taylor insisted that we learned many Bible passages off by heart, so that we could *give a reason for the hope* that was within us.' This hope was to stand Dolly in good stead through the events that followed.

Wally told how 'The hamlet of Dunks Green held attraction for me for more than one reason as I grew older, for in the houses known as Rabbit Hutch Row lived the Coppins family. They attended the chapel with regularity.' Indeed, Dolly had begun to attend more regularly following the family tragedy which had cut deeply into her life.

Her working life was cut short by the untimely death of her mother Mary. Mary had gone into hospital to give birth to twins, one of whom died in hospital. Mary herself was never to come home again. After being in hospital for three months she passed away, leaving one baby, four young boys and a younger sister to be taken care of. Dolly had to come home and take up domestic duties there. A neighbour looked after baby Michael for a while before Nell and Dolly decided to take him back into the family. Nell, being the older sister, was in charge at first, but soon she moved out to get married and produce a baby of her own. Dolly was left to finish bringing up the boys and her younger sister Freda. How did she cope? Whatever her feelings at the time, Dolly, in later years, would confess that she had never been disappointed that she hadn't had a son of her own. She had had her fill of bringing up boys!

A further blow fell on to Dolly and the rest of the family when Michael died of meningitis at the age of eight. His brother Gordon remembers how Michael had been ill all night, but that Dolly had made Gordon go to school in the morning. When he got home he found that his younger brother had died.

His description of Dolly is that she was 'a very strong person. She put up with a lot all through the years. She was very strict; she had to be; there was always a stick nearby. She was very strong-willed as a result of looking after the boys. They always did as she told them or woe betide!'

'I don't know how we survived,' added Gordon. 'We were a rough lot; it was a hard life. Dolly did all the donkey work.' Indeed, Dolly had to go to work in the fields, doing jobs such as potato picking, as well as look after the family. She would sometimes have to take the children with her, pushing two in the pram, with two walking at either side.

Someone had given Dolly a sewing machine, for which she was very thankful. After working in the fields all day she would sit up late into the night, struggling to make trousers for the boys out of old overcoats which other people had given her, no doubt doing their best to help the young bereft family. She had no pattern for the trousers and she would tell how they were so difficult to make that it would take her hours to master how to do it by copying from the boys' old clothes. But, though she would weep over them, she persevered out of necessity. She remembered writing notes on old sugar bags, writing paper being a luxury she could not afford.

'It was a wonder some of the boys didn't end up in a home and all stayed together,' Nell remarked. 'She was the boss. What Dolly said went! We all worked in the fields in the summer, but the boys were free, picking apples, strawberries and raspberries, hops. Up early in the morning and back late in the evening.'

The lady next door to the Coppins family used to feel sorry for Gordon on Saturday mornings because Dolly would send everyone outside whilst she cleaned the floors. He would stand outside shouting, 'Dolly can I come in!' until the neighbour took pity on him and let him into her house.

Latterly, when it was put to Gordon that Dolly had never talked much about her younger days, he remarked,

'They weren't happy memories, a lot of them; best forgotten.' Though Dolly was a disciplinarian in those difficult days, out of necessity, Gordon remembers that 'She always had a kiss for us whenever we went anywhere. We didn't go hungry and I enjoyed my childhood.'

It seems that Dolly had won the respect of her neighbours when they saw her taking her charges to Sunday School. She certainly caught Wally's eye. Eventually the North family were to move into the same row of houses as the Coppins family. Wally gleefully recounted:

'Dolly and I were now living within a hundred yards of each other.'

'She was greatly admired by us all,' he said, 'especially Mr Taylor, who spoke most highly of her, not least for the fact that, when we held an open-air meeting in front of her house, she would come out and stand with the church and testify in a loud, clear voice to her faith in Christ, before her family, neighbours and friends. I became very attracted to her, though it was years before I asked her to become my wife. A measure of her devotion to Christ may be gauged from her answer to my request:~' I will go home and pray about it.'

She must have said yes, for they were married in 1941. They had a simple wedding at the chapel. Dolly had borrowed a wedding dress for the occasion. It was war time, the Second World War having broken out in 1939, rationing was in force and there were no spare coupons for dresses. But, because the bride's brother had just died, she did not wear the borrowed dress and the whole thing was a rather subdued affair. However, they did have a honeymoon. Someone had offered the newly-weds the use of their house in London and, despite the fact that London was being heavily bombed, they took up the offer and had a holiday.

To Dolly's delight, after her marriage to Wally, the family was allocated a new house with a bath and a copper [boiler] inside for the washing. Luxuries indeed for the young housewife! By this time Dolly's father had remarried, but his new wife was not very popular with the children. So the young couple began married life still looking after some of Dolly's siblings. Gordon says that Wally had asked them if they would like to go into Barnardo's [children's care home], but they said No. 'No more was said about it,' remembers Gordon. Perhaps Wally was reluctant to share his home with the boys. He had not been altogether popular with his new wife's family.

'He was from London, and he was always studying and reading,' says sister Nell. 'They thought he was a show-off and cocky! He was a boss and they didn't like it. Perhaps they weren't all that excited. They had to behave a bit better. I know they didn't like Wally very much. They didn't want to be bossed about. He was clever. He would never come down to their level. He was good at sport and they were not. He was a know-all and a bit better than they were.' Later on, though, relationships must have improved as, in due course, Wally went into business with Dolly's brothers.

Of course Dolly had not been the only girl interested in the talented young preacher. She would tell her children how a close friend of hers would not speak to her after she and Wally began courting!

Engagement picture

Wedding day 1941 with respective fathers and brother in law, Alf Bathurst as Best Man

With Mrs Milner on their 25th wedding anniversary

50th wedding anniversary with their three daughters

CHAPTER 3
A PREACHER TRANSFORMED

'THE GREATEST MOMENT OF MY LIFE'

During the time when Wally and Dolly were courting a travelling evangelist and his wife, Mr and Mrs Saxby, came and pitched their tent in the village of Plaxtol. Mrs. Saxby was crippled with a disease, contracted when they had been missionaries in Angola, and was mostly confined to a wheelchair.

The chapel people were delighted to support the evangelistic meetings and to hear the Gospel preached with power in their village. One of the souls converted at the time was Dolly's father, who, though attending chapel and seeing to it that his children did too, was not a saved man. One particular evening, as the sermon ended, the congregation became aware of a disturbing noise. Describing it to his nieces many years later, Dolly's brother Gordon recounted,

'Grandad Coppins came straight out of the pub into the mission tent, pitched behind The Rifleman, and got himself saved!'

'I turned around,' said Wally, when retelling this episode, 'and saw my future father-in-law in what seemed to me to be great distress. He was; he was under conviction of sin. When he left the tent he was a saved man. It was the first time I had seen and heard such a conversion. God opened my eyes as well as the eyes of my father-in law to be. It was life-changing. Though I had been a believer from an early age and God had kept me from much evil; though I had attended church and heard much preaching, I had never been convicted of sin, nor had I seen anyone else under conviction of sin nor saved from it.

That fact did not greatly concern me. I was a believer; I had always been a believer. I was a church worker of no mean accomplishment and I believed I was a sinner. Of course! Wasn't everyone a sinner? It was not until much later that I learned that it was possible to live on this earth and not be a sinner; but a saint. I had never heard it once suggested that I could be free from sin, as Paul so clearly states [Romans 6]. But the advent of Mr and Mrs Saxby soon changed all that, at least for me, if not for everybody.

One day I was standing with others outside the Chapel when Mrs Saxby came up to me and said,

"Do you know what you want?"

"No!"

"You need to ask God for a new heart, filled with the Holy Ghost."

To the best of my recollection I was dumbstruck. I never said a word; no-one had ever spoken to me like that before. I was a Christian, wasn't I? A believer, a preacher, a Bible reader, a good person? I never drank or smoked or swore, or went to the pictures, or kept company with those that did these things. What was wrong with me? What she was saying did not fit in with my beliefs and doctrine. I rejected it, or at least thought I did. But I hadn't.

At the time I was getting invitations to go out preaching and I well remember one Sunday, when I arrived home from a preaching engagement I went to visit Dolly, to whom I was engaged. She was greatly moved when I began to weep and, putting her arms around me, asked me what was the matter. With shame I confessed to her,

"I am the contradiction of all that I preach!"

For the first time in my life I was under conviction of sin – not of the sins I had committed, which I am sure were many, but of the heart disease of Sin, from which all my sins in thought, word and deed flowed. Not long after that I did exactly as that precious lady Mrs Saxby had said. After wrestling with denials and warnings from others, one Saturday night by my bedside I asked God for and received both a clean heart from God and the Holy Spirit.

I was born again. I became a new person. I knew because I became so different from what I had been before. My testimony had always been what I *believed*; now it became what I *was*. To quote Paul –*By the grace of God I am what I am* –.With regard to one's own experience, quotations from Scripture are good, but statements of one's own condition, expressed in one's own words, are better.

It was the greatest moment of my life; my most treasured memory. I began to live the new life. Oh, it was wonderful! It still is. All the struggle to live the Christian life ceased. I was able to live free from sin, exactly as Paul said I should. A goal had been reached. What lay ahead?'

DIFFICULT TIMES

After this transforming experience, things began to be difficult at the chapel. Wally recalled,

'The fact that I had transacted with God to receive a new heart was not well received by Mr. Taylor. His doctrine did not allow for it. His teaching was that a man must receive Jesus Christ as Saviour and grow in grace and the knowledge of Jesus Christ. I heard him say that the text in Ezekiel about the gift of a new heart was for Israel only and was not for today. Therefore, when I began to speak of a new heart and a new spirit, he was displeased.

A local Brother [he belonged to the Plymouth Brethren] who used to speak to us occasionally and was highly thought of, told me that he had heard that Wally North had received the Second Blessing. His manner was frankly disapproving, but I had not so much as heard of the phrase. One thing, which, at the time, I dismissed, but which had a fuller meaning for me later, was the remark made by our pastor when he heard of my experience:-

"He's only just been converted!"

Later I was to discover that Mrs. Saxby, the lady who had pointed me towards the Baptism in the Spirit [a phrase she did not herself use] was a Holiness believer. That is: she believed in the doctrine of Second Blessing Holiness. She believed this to be what the Bible itself teaches and gave uncompromising testimony to it. Whatever the truth of that I did not know, but I certainly knew I needed a clean heart and to be filled with the Spirit and I had no doubt that this is what had happened to me. I read books appropriate to the teaching of Entire Sanctification; books for which I thank God, and which I recommend to any seeking holiness of life, *without which no man shall see the Lord.*'

Wally said that, as a consequence of all this, people in the chapel began to look at him 'askance', but he could not remember anyone asking him for an explanation of what had happened to him. He says,

'The Holy Ghost was not talked about in our church. Except for the weekly benediction and at Whitsuntide, the blessed Third person of the Trinity was hardly mentioned although we were periodically reminded that the Scriptures were given by inspiration of God. At times we were told that He came to glorify Christ, though in what way we were left to imagine. The main emphasis was upon the Lord Jesus and His work, with a few references to the fruit of the Spirit. To the best of my recollection the Gifts of the Spirit were never mentioned. One sorrowful phrase stands out in my memory – NOT FOR TODAY - , three deadly words which closed the whole subject to my enquiring mind.'

Knowing what he had sought and received from the Lord, Wally began to preach this Holiness teaching. Because of this he found himself in immediate trouble with his church, which resulted in his being publicly denounced from the platform in front of a full congregation.

'It was a harrowing time,' Wally recalls, 'but God brought me through it with the beginnings of the doctrine of Second Blessing Holiness strongly formulating in my mind. None of these things moved me and I went on in the conviction that God had entirely sanctified me that night at my bedside.'

FOR CONSCIENCE SAKE

After their war time wedding Wally and Dolly settled into their house at *The Spout* in Plaxtol. These were dangerous times in rural Kent; Wally's parents had had part of their house roof blown away. But the danger did not deter the newly-weds from walking to Tonbridge, a distance of about five miles, to meet with Mr. and Mrs. Saxby and learn more about Holiness. They had to wear tin hats for protection and sometimes they had to duck down in the ditches when bombers flew overhead towards London.

Life was far from easy. The couple were still looking after some of Dolly's brothers and her younger sister Freda when their first baby, Judith, came along in 1942. They gave her the middle name of May, after Mrs. Saxby, now affectionately known as Auntie May. [After her husband's death Auntie May would come and visit the family, now living in Bradford. The three children remember that she would never travel by bus on a Sunday, making things a bit difficult for their parents].

During the war, and for several years afterwards, there were many food shortages. Every member of every family was issued with a ration book giving precise details of certain types of food which they were allowed during one week. The new baby meant that the family were allocated rations for an extra person. Wally grew all the vegetables in the garden.

With the Second World War came conscription and, being a man of military age, Wally was called up for service. Not everyone had to go to war, of course. Age, sickness, work of national importance and various other classes of exemption were recognised. Among them were people who conscientiously objected to war, commonly called Conscies, or C.O.s. Being one of these, Wally registered the fact at the local office and awaited the tribunal. During the waiting period, he was made the leader of a fire-watching team. This was an obligatory duty in an area in danger of being bombed because it was on the direct route to London for German planes. Wally relates:

'When the day for my hearing arrived I went to Maidstone, the county town. Three solemn-looking men sat on the Bench; a judge, a psychiatrist and a trade union official. When my name was called I stepped up to the Bench, made my statement, was questioned about it, was asked if I had any objections to land work, to which I answered No, was assigned to the Hampshire War Agricultural Committee and was dismissed. The whole procedure was over in ten minutes and I was treated with complete fairness.'

Wally was thankful to God and very relieved that he had not been shut in, nor sent to prison, nor ordered to work in the mines. Instead he was ordered to go to Hampshire and, after going home to tell his parents and Dolly the verdict, prepared to leave. He became one of a company of men, living in caravans and working on various farms in the county. Their job was land reclamation, 'hedging and ditching'. Ditching was reclaiming unused, water logged fields for use in crop growing. During the war every inch of ground had to be made usable; dereliction, neglect and wastage had to become productive. 'It was hard work and rightly so,' was Wally's verdict.

He discovered a group of men who were members of a Methodist based society, calling themselves The Fellowship of Reconciliation. The name attracted him and he applied for and was accepted into membership.

'The Fellowship of Reconciliation proved to be a motley crowd,' he wrote. 'I very soon found that C.O.s [Conscientious Objectors] were a mixed bag indeed. I suppose I was very naïve, but it came to me almost as a shock to discover that the Fellowship of Reconciliation included all sorts of men, holding very different convictions about objections to war, as different as their faces differed. I soon found that politics played a large part in most of their minds. One man actually assured me that if the right government was in, "I would shove a knife between your shoulders today!" He was a university man, extremely well-spoken, a thorough gentleman; but a self-confessed potential murderer; otherwise he was quite friendly!'

A Jewish man, converted to Christ, was amongst the people Wally met at the Fellowship. He was a Pentecostal and he and Wally became close friends. At first Wally viewed him with suspicion as he 'spoke with tongues'.

'I had been taught that this was well-nigh Satanic,' Wally said, 'but when I opened my Bible to read he joined me and listened to me. We shared some precious times together.' But Wally had to move on and the friendship was short lived, though significant in Wally's spiritual education.

When Wally, having grown tired of hedging and ditching, applied for a transfer to the forestry division, he was surprised to find that the bosses had been about to make him into a foreman. He had become friendly with the previous foreman, helping him with the plans given him by the overseers, which he had difficulty in understanding. Because of this inefficiency the bosses had decided to give Wally the job. But Wally had been visiting the foreman's home with him at weekends and had gone to the Methodist church with him and his family, and though it would have meant higher wages and less work, Wally refused this 'totally unexpected' promotion and took up forestry. This job was to provide training for his future business.

Wally now became one of a group living in a house in the forest. There he met a man who lived in Tonbridge and cycled to work every day, a distance of about twenty miles. Plaxtol was only another five miles further than Tonbridge, so Wally decided to start cycling to and fro. Each day, therefore, saw him cycling fifty miles as well as working for twelve hours. He scorned the idea of being tired.

'I was young and strong,' he said. 'Indeed, on some Sundays I used to cycle to Tonbridge to preach.' Besides, now he could see Dolly every day and that made up for all the hard work. God was looking after them even through difficult times.

FIRE WATCHING

Five days after his first child Judith was born in May 1942, Wally was given his 'Certificate of Registration in Register of Conscientious Objectors' under the National Service Acts. But he was not out of the woods yet. Later in the same year it became compulsory to register under the Civil Defence Duties Order for fire watching duties. Though already taking part in these services voluntarily, Wally refused to register. In a letter to the Clerk of the Council, dated 1-4-43, he stated: 'It is being involved in this necessary part of the war machine to which I object.'

The Fire Guard Staff Officer advised him: 'Your deliberate refusal to register under the above order is a very serious matter.' Wally replied, 'I quite understand the seriousness of the step I am taking, but, being assured of will, the consequences do not matter. God's word to me is plain, and, being in receipt of the same, I have no other desire but to obey Him in this, as in any other particular of life.' The following is a copy of the statement Wally made to F.J. Baden-Fuller, Fire Guard Staff Officer for the Council:-

'I herewith return enclosed form unsigned, for as one who has been born again [John 3-3] and is conscious of the claims God has upon all He has thus regenerated, by virtue of the *precious blood of Christ* and the power of the Holy Spirit, I have, by His grace, submitted my whole self, body, soul and spirit to Him. Thus, living *by the faith of the Son of God, who loved me and gave Himself for me [Gal. 2, 2]* I know of a surety that God's will for me is not in this thing. Therefore, I refuse to become involved by giving my signature to the necessary forms. Yours faithfully...'

In reply, the Council decided to take proceedings against him and Wally was summonsed to appear before the justices at West Malling, where he was given a three month jail sentence.

IN JAIL

A police sergeant duly turned up one day on the family's doorstep to arrest Wally and deliver him to Maidstone Jail for his allotted sentence. A knock came at the door and Dolly opened it. She knew the policeman had come to arrest her husband.

'He stood on the doorstep and read out the warrant "...Go to prison for two months..."' Wally recounted at Auchenheath.

"Beg your pardon; that warrant's wrong!"

"I know it is. I was duty sergeant at the court the morning your case came in. I know they gave you three months, but it says two months here and that's all I can take you for."

'So God had overruled,' said Wally. 'A third gone straight away! So we said, "Come in." We had a chat. Dolly made the sergeant a cup of tea whilst I was getting changed.' Dolly went to the door with the baby in her arms and they had a little prayer before Wally got into the car. As they were driving to the prison the police officer said,

"I can't make you out. I've had to arrest many people and I've never seen anything like this." Wally's reply was,

"Well, we both know we're doing God's will. There's nothing to worry about."

"Good luck!" were the sergeant's words when he delivered his prisoner at the gate.

NUMBER B119

G.W.'s remark at Auchenheath in 1975, when telling this story, was,

'The older I get the more objection I take to war, the more deep-rooted it is in my heart. But this I determined in prison; whatever they did to me I was going to master my Bible.'

He commented on the fact that he was so green that when they asked him, "Convicted or remand?" he didn't know what they were talking about and replied,

"By the law, but not by God!"

"Army, Navy, Air force?"

"No."

"Conscie?"

"Yes."

"Worst of the lot! Come here!"

'I was pushed into the worst cell,' Wally went on, 'where somebody had been so ill they had taken him to the hospital, where he later died. It was filthy. That's our country for you. Whatever you do stay out of prison; because if you go to prison just a petty thief, by the time you come out you'll know how to crack every safe in the country. That's where they learn it. I knew how to break a safe. I've never done it. You go in not too bad and come out thoroughly rotten!'

Wally felt that he was favoured by God in prison because he had been on the block for only one night when he realised that someone was trying to communicate with him. 'He must have known how green I was,' Wally commented. 'The next morning, as I was going out of my cell, he said to me, "I'm going out tomorrow. Want a job? I'm a wing orderly. Like me to put your number up for it?"

At night time, when it came to serving the meals, the officer came to unlock the door and said, "B119, come on. Duty!" I had to hold the basket while he doled out at every cell door. Then at the end he gave me extra. So right then, at the beginning, you see how God looked after me. When they dished out the porridge in the morning, everyone else got one ladle; I got two. I hadn't asked for it. As wing orderly, when they dished out the tea and they came to your cell, you put out your drinking cup, but the officers put your glass out as well. So you had your drinking glass and your teacup full. You had twice as much.'

PREACHING IN PRISON

An Irishman, also a C.O., and a Brethren believer, befriended Wally. Wally described him as, 'a lovely little fellow, but he couldn't preach for toffee nuts. He was ever so small and I could hardly understand him. He had a weak heart and the Army wouldn't have had him anyway, but he stood by what he believed.' During exercise periods this Irishman would gather the men together and Wally would preach to them as they walked round the yard. He described the scene,

'I had the glorious privilege of walking round the prison preaching as though I was in an open-air meeting; God did work in prison; the needs were great.' He remembered a sneering remark by the prison chaplain, who hadn't himself had to fight,

'I don't mind fighting so that people like you needn't fight.'

MAIL BAGS.

At that time prisoners were set the task of sewing ropes into mailbags. One morning when Wally was in the bag shop, learning how to sew eight stitches to the inch, an officer came in and wrote on his slate, 7BAGS PER NIGHT, OR ELSE! But Wally was determined to spend time in prison waiting on God and getting to know the Bible, so he stitched only three ropes. When he had done these he left the work and took up his Bible, which had been returned to him, together with a photo of his wife and daughter, when he came into jail. He remarked,

'It was their fault. They shouldn't have given it to me. I took my Bible and knelt by my bed. They lifted up the peepholes and looked in at me. They saw me disobeying their orders and I didn't care. I used prison to wait on God. I understood Romans in Maidstone Jail – good place to be taught the truth – I understood the first epistle of Peter in Maidstone Jail. That's what happened.'

As for the mail bags, Wally sewed them so well that the bag shop man put his work on exhibition.

'Because I did it unto Jesus,' said Wally, 'I sewed mail bags as though they were taking letters to the throne.'

After serving his six week sentence, the prisoner was released. He remembered, 'When I came out I could have wept for joy. I went inside in midwinter and it was spring when I came out. It was lovely, wonderful!' Having been imprisoned for failing to sign fire-watching papers, Wally promptly helped put out a fire near to his home.

LETTERS FROM JAIL

_ To his surprise, Wally was allowed to write three letters home on prison notepaper; Dolly kept them for the rest of her life. Some extracts from these are revealing of her husband's state of mind during his short sentence.

1st **letter :** -'Saw the assistant chaplain yesterday. He talked about everything but the Saviour – such a pity, for there's plenty of scope for evangelisation here. Already the Lord has enabled me to contact one or two chaps [during exercise spells] who definitely admit consciousness of sin committed and the need felt for a different life. Pray, dear, that the Lord Himself shall so indwell and empower me by the Holy Spirit that even here I may be able to witness to Him as the Redeemer and Saviour of men – to his glory alone. He continues to supply my daily need as I draw upon Him, and what more could I ask?

You know, dear, when Paul said, *in whatsoever state I am therewith to be content*, he wrote from prison. Perhaps such an experience as this is necessary for full enjoyment of the living Christ; for, after but a few days here, the new and unfamiliar way of life supplied me with many new and grand ways of proving the Blessed Lord's presence.'

From the same letter: –'With conscience clear and a true conviction of being in the will of the Lord, there is nothing to fear and I know that you are being well provided for by a loving Heavenly Father, so what matters? Isn't it lovely to have so much space in which to write? I am most agreeably surprised, I can tell you.

Shall be reading in Romans 8 tonight – glorious chapter – *led of the Spirit* –*walking in the Spirit* – *the glorious liberty of the sons of God* – truly, as S.C.S. says, *Four walls do not a prison make, nor iron bars a cage.* - . Do you know dear, even my little window, set high in the wall, causes me to think of Him who is coming again, for I have to look up all the time. But for a grey wall and a few bars, my view is of Heaven always.

All my love, thoughts and prayers. Hope Judith can walk now. After removing all the notes from my Bible the officer handed it back to me, together with Judith's photo, and there she is now, staring in wonder at her strangely-garbed Daddad from her position precariously fixed above the mirror, bless her! I don't know, but I should think you could bring her in to see me when you come. I'll have to make enquiries.

Read 1 Peter carefully, my sweet. It's so true and beautiful to me right now.'

2nd letter 'I've had many opportunities for talks during exercise times and have noted with dismay the awful and inexcusable lack of knowledge on the part of all and sundry of the teaching of the Book – the way of salvation. Indeed, the very men [this prison contains the major part servicemen] that are supposed to be fighting for a Christian country to put the world to right, know little or nothing of Christ at all. There is a golden chance of proclaiming the Gospel here, but so far as I can ascertain, the men who have that chance waste it. I wonder if it has ever crossed their minds that *After death cometh the judgement* and *Every man shall give an account of himself to God.*

Since I last wrote, I have been taken from the mailbag shop and placed in No.2 Party - cleaners. We scrub floors, wash paint, clean out empty cells etc. and, in between times, lug in coal and coke. Everybody in the party is pretty certain he is developing housemaids' knee and swears he'll never look a flannel or bucket in the eye upon departure. My suggestion was that I'd send my wife out to work and do the housework myself. – Think it over, dear!

The change of party does not mean no bags to sew – O, no! Putting one in the bag shop is merely to train one for an endless succession of bags to occupy one's leisure hours. Still, it's all part of the authorities' delightful plans for reforming bad characters!

In this letter Wally refers to 'Un-neighbourly remarks from Mrs. G.' and urges his wife not to let them upset her. Also, 'Tell Maud to buck up,' as his sister was understandably upset at his going to prison.

Giving instructions to Dolly as to how to get to the prison with his mother and daughter on visiting day, he directs her past 'a big, thick grey wall, about 25 feet high, which I see every day – that's the wall I've either got to push over or walk up or burrow through if ever I attempt to come home before my two months are up. I'll have my best grey suit on and try to be clean shaven to kiss my dear wife and daughter. Oh, I do hope she'll recognise me. I'm taking it for granted you will! When you think that some chaps in here are serving up to 12 years, what are two months? And it's not as though it's with a sense of guilt, praise God. I'm happy in Him and, as this is of His all wise will, there are no regrets. There is one brother in here with whom I have complete fellowship – we are one in Christ Jesus. Remember him in prayer, dear. He's a great soul.'

3rd **Letter.** After visiting day, Wally expressed his delight at seeing his family –'The visit was a real thrill, and the fact that dear little J.M. remembered her daddy was especially gratifying – a real oasis in a dry and dreary desert.

My little pal [the Irishman] has left me – gone to a better part of the prison. Of course, the fact that he has departed now leaves me without a special envoy for the remaining days, but it also widens the horizon of my opportunities for contact with others who know not our Lord Jesus Christ. Only today, I found that a faithful witness to the truth of salvation proved very attractive to the most unlikely of fellows, and I'm positive that there is still a willingness to hear on the part of the uninitiated, providing the simple truth and the bald facts are honestly presented.

Instead of people hedging and keeping clear of me when they know the brand of conversation I deal in, I find a spirit of enquiry and attentiveness. I'm sure that the facts of Salvation as given in the Word are absolutely strange to the majority of fellows in this prison. Talks with them reveal that the Hail-fellow-well-met neo-political sermons, so frequently indulged in from the pulpit today, cut no ice. Tell them of a Saviour who *saves to the uttermost all that come unto God by Him*, and their interest is kindled. I definitely know of one case of confessed blessing after a chat or two, and that is sufficient repayment in itself, should nothing else come of it all.

Sunday is the one day in the whole week that drags. Since being in here I've read practically the whole of the New Testament, with no little profit and blessing to my own soul. There's nothing like saturating the mind in Scripture to buoy one up even when the downcast spirit sinks under depressing circumstances.

– There'll be so much to recount to each other when I get home that there'll be no work done next Tuesday. There's such a lot to say. For instance, I must hear the full story of the miraculous way that the Lord has blessed and provided for you. The things you have put in black and white have thrilled me, so doubtless, the whole will fill me with wonder and praise.'

Wally remarks that there were so few prisoners in Maidstone Jail at the time that, 'There'll be some unemployed prison authorities about soon. I'll have to do my best to keep them in a job, eh?' He is eagerly anticipating his return home and finishes,

'Tell J.M. to try and walk to meet her daddy when he arrives.'

'P.S. I shall receive my first week's wages on Monday and promise to bring it all home to you – thirty one and a half pence!'

IN DISGRACE

Although Wally obviously felt that he had benefited from his prison experiences and looked back on them at Auchenheath as part of what 'made him tick', it is clear from his letters that the family, as well as himself, had had to suffer because of his actions. They had had to share in his disgrace, whilst perhaps not sharing his views or the convictions which carried him through. They had to put up with the taunts of other villagers and they felt it deeply. As well as this, Dolly was left with an eleven month old baby, without her means of support. Wally himself had to face the cold shoulders of the villagers when he resumed his farm work after coming out of prison.

'He used to drive a lorry on the farm,' remembers Dolly's brother Gordon, 'and drop the women at various points for work. A lot of the women wouldn't go with him because he was a Conscie. People in the village were against him. You could understand that because their husbands were away in the army.'

That reflected on the rest of the family. One of Dolly's brothers was in the army so one can imagine the turmoil her husband's stand brought about. Dolly's Uncle had won the Victoria Cross in the Great War, so he must have been regarded as a hero. Her father had been in the army and Wally's father would have been, had his sight not been so bad, so it is obvious that none of them shared his position.

PATRIOTISM IS A FALSE GOD

Many years later, in response to requests to do so, GW. set down his reasons for being a C.O. The article is entitled 'For conscience sake', and he begins by saying that he sought 'no quarrel with anyone on this matter, because every Christian has to face this out with God. My objective is to help every one to do that.' He goes on:

'In my formative years the bravest man I knew was a Conscientious Objector. I am glad I met him. I owe him much.' This undoubtedly refers to his old pastor, Edwin Taylor. He continues:

'It is often thought, if not said, that C.O.s are cowards; but this man was bold and fearless; a fighter for truth, if ever there was one. It is not the easiest thing to stand upon convictions of truth in a hostile climate, as I soon learned. During the Great [First World] War it was not unusual to pick up white feathers [signifying cowardice] from the doormat. Both my Uncle and father served in World War One, and, though I was never told so, the family felt the disgrace of my stand.'

He asserts that his objection to taking part in warfare was based on Scripture, not just on conscience, 'as this is not a sure guide on this or any other spiritual matter.' Here he makes a statement on which much of his teaching rests, - 'Arguably, the greatest charge which could be brought against modern churches is that they do not know to which Covenant they belong.' This refers to the fact that God had ordered His people to do battle in the Old Testament, though not in the New.

His first argument is that Jesus did not allow His servants to fight and that 'God's kingdom on earth today is exclusively a spiritual kingdom. Patriotism is a false God and a very cruel one too; the worship of one's country is idolatry. The flower of the world's manhood has been sacrificed on its altars.'

His second argument stems from the fact of the Body of Christ [1 Corinthians 12]:

'If Christ and His body are one, then Christ and every member of that body are one. It is no worse to attempt to destroy the body of Christ wholly, by crucifixion, than to attempt to do so piecemeal. How dare one member of His body do anything to another member because he belongs to another nation or race? The regenerate German or Russian, or Chinese, or African is more my brother than my own kith and kin, if she or he is not regenerate.'

When, in later life, G.W. often visited and ministered in Germany, he was very glad that he had never taken up arms against the German people, his beloved brothers and sisters. He states here that 'It is quite inconceivable that anyone should believe it possible to go with a gun, dealing death to people and later go with a Bible, offering life to them.'

He points out that: 'Conscientious Objection is a large umbrella – humanists, pacifists, anti-government agitators and many others find themselves protection under it. We do not belong to them. These things are not primarily a question of conscientious objection, but of spiritual conviction.'

He asserts that, 'To be a bearer of the Good News, a man's life must be consistent with the teachings of Jesus as a whole. Jesus said that they who live by the sword will perish by the sword. He also told us to love our enemies, to do good to them which hate us and to pray for them that despitefully use us. I have never heard that taught by military authority – Rather to the contrary.'

He discovered that in Nazi Germany there had been at least one concentration camp for conscientious objectors – 'It is to be presumed that these persons were treated like the inmates of other concentration camps and died rather than do anything to further the war effort.'

He tells the story of how he was called one day to visit a retired army colonel and tried to bring him the word of God. The colonel told him, 'It's alright for you. I have had to order hundreds of men to their deaths.' G.W. replied,

'God can forgive even that.' Nothing he said seemed to reach the soldier and, 'He was a sad, tormented man, battling with his conscience, finding no way of peace or way of escape. Small comfort to him, or to others like him, to say, "*I only did my duty.*" Let us ask ourselves this question: "If Jesus was on earth today and war broke out, which uniform would he wear and whose side would He take?"'

Although G.W. stated that he believed the things said here were part of the Gospel message of, *love your enemies,* he also said that he did not intend them to be a criticism of anybody.

'If a man, being a Christian, becomes party to mass or individual killing through warfare because he thought he was doing right at the time, or because he was wrongly taught by his spiritual leaders or teachers, there is forgiveness with God,' he says.

In spite of his strong views on this controversial subject, G.W. retained many, no doubt gracious and forgiving friends with differing views, notable among them being Major Leonard Moules of W.E.C. fame. Having many things in common, the friendship was warm between the two men. Indeed, when W.E.C. [Worldwide Evangelisation Crusade] were considering buying their Bulstrode premises, the two men went together to look at the building, and prayed there that God would use it for His glory.

GOING INTO BUSINESS

Life returned to normal following prison and war work. Dolly's father put up some money and a family forestry business began, no doubt inspired, at least in part, by Wally's experiences with the War Ag. Department. Dolly's brothers and Wally founded the business, which continued for many years after he had left it. Wally said that, 'God prospered it tremendously.' Others came into the flourishing business. G.W. pointed out that it was founded on 'absolute righteousness'. A government representative down from Whitehall was told by another wood trader, 'This is the only honest woodsman I know.'

Talking to young people present at Auchenheath, G.W. pointed out,

'If they bought 100 stakes, we gave them 105. They were wealthy; we were struggling in those days; but we gave them more than they paid for, until God, in the end, established it, because of its sheer basic honesty and righteousness.'

Dolly sometimes used to go out into the woods too, taking the baby with her. Wally was physically as 'strong as an ox. He would think nothing of getting hold of a nine-foot pit prop,' remembers brother-in-law Gordon. Indeed the strength in his arms, perhaps gained by chopping so many trees, remained throughout his life, probably maintained through waving his arms about when preaching!

He could never understand it when young people complained of being tired. 'We never got tired,' he would say. 'We started at 6 in the morning. I'd come home and sit in a chair. Dolly'd have a meal ready for me. I'd put my feet up. She'd undo my shoes. I'd have a tray here for my food; a Bible propped up there. I'd get up and change; go out to preach. I devoured that Bible. There were times when my wife used to say to me,

"Dear, put that Bible away. It's not fair." I used to hold the baby; I didn't know whether she was falling out of my arms or not. So I used to shut the Book.'

At Auchenheath, when relating this part of the story, G.W. paused to say,

'It isn't all Bible, of course; but let me tell you – that Bible – I lived for it. I mastered it until it mastered me. If you want to know how I tick, I'm telling you. You don't get it any other way.'

Perhaps surprisingly, G.W. never recommended Bible Colleges to young people. 'They can help; they can hinder,' was his opinion. Coming from a working-class family, and having had no opportunity for higher education, he was always surprised by the fact that so many well-educated people wanted to listen to him.

'I thank God for training me through many men and many experiences [none of them formal]' he said.

GW.'s lack of formal education was sometimes surprising to his hearers, because he spoke with an accent much more refined than his East End background may have suggested. He insisted that he had deliberately worked on his accent because he wanted to be clearly understood. He certainly never seemed to be lacking in knowledge, though he claimed not to have read many books other than the Bible. Indeed, during his Bradford pastorate, some members of the congregation would complain that he sounded 'posh' and that they had difficulty in understanding the long words he used!

Back in Plaxtol, working by day and preaching in the evenings and at weekends, Wally knew that he was coming to a division in the way. He was running a Bible study class near to his home and he recalled sadly,

'My dear, dear mother and father wouldn't walk a hundred yards to come to it because I talked about Baptism in the Spirit. That's what prejudice can do. They're both with the Lord, bless them!'

PAYING THE PRICE.–FIRST PASTORATE

'Either the ministry or the business had to go,' Wally stated. And, when he was asked to take on a Baptist church at Loose in 1946 he knew it was time to leave Plaxtol. It was an independent church, not attached to any Union, in a beautiful valley near Maidstone, the county town of Kent. Anita Neale, who was 17 at the time, remembers that at the service, 'when Mr. North came *on trial*' she couldn't remember the contents of his sermon, but, 'It fed my soul, and I wanted more,' she says.

'Mr North agreed to become our pastor, but there was something he wanted to tell us first – he had been in prison! There was a hush at first. He explained he was a C.O.

Question – Did we still want him as Pastor? Answer – Definitely yes!

A Preacher Transformed

So began 6 years of ministry in which souls were saved and many of us led into the things of the Holy Spirit. Loose Baptist is an evangelical church and we loved the Word of God. Mr. North brought a new emphasis, as he majored on teaching about Holiness and Sanctification. He started a meeting for those who wanted to go on with God and called it *Improvers*. There were about 5 of us, mixed in age. We met in a small room, which had been the kitchen of the church, to save fuel. It was that time; after the war. We were there in 1947 all huddled around one small gas fire. I remember getting chilblains on my ankles!'

G.W. himself described the time when he was called to go to Loose. He left the business, taking nothing from it. By this time the family had grown to two children aged 2 and 4; a third baby was on the way.

'The only way I could go into the ministry,' said G.W., 'was that we should be divided.' Unfortunately, at the time there was not a home available for the family, so Dolly and the two children stayed with her mother-in-law and Wally went off to Loose. This was, of course, a very difficult time for the family, especially Dolly. It was the only time that any of the children could remember seeing their mother crying.

'But we knew the call of God,' explained G.W. At Auchenheath. 'I tell you, if you want to know how to tick, you've got to pay the price.'

'There's no light way, you've got to pay the price,' he repeated. The baby, a third baby girl, was born whilst the couple were still separated; but finally,- 'God found us a house. We all came together again – a long and wonderful story.' The house was in a single crescent of homes, built for special council workers. The Norths were not entitled to one of these, but there was much rejoicing when they finally settled. Anita Neale recounts some of her recollections of Wally's first pastorate.

'Mr. North started a Junior Fellowship for children in the village and took over being Sunday School Superintendent. He led open-air meetings on the village green with our Witness Team. He introduced us to tithing and stopped having a collection plate taken round in the services. Mr. North led my mother and the mothers of two of my friends from the Chapel to the Lord. The Lord brought some families in. People began to come to the Lord to know Him as Saviour during 1948/49. Mr. North had witnessed to people in his road, and two men, about his own age, were saved.' The Witness Team used to get on their bikes and cycle to the hop-gardens for open-air meetings, witnessing to the Londoners who came annually to Kent to pick the hops, just as Wally had done as a child.

It was during this time in Loose that Wally came into contact with a young man called David Wetherly. He used to come and visit from Dartford and was so keen for others to come and hear the truth that he brought crowds of young people with him. Wally was thrilled with all the spiritual hunger, but their physical hunger was more of a problem to Dolly! She had to feed them every Saturday, before the prayer, praise and testimony meetings. But God was moving and many souls were saved and continued in the Christian life.

NOT FOR TODAY

Anita Neale remembers an 'important time in Mr. North's ministry.' It came about through his contact with the Medway Towns Missions conference. One of the missions was at Gillingham Salem Calvary Holiness Church. Wally went along to join in the evangelistic campaign there. He was preaching Holiness at the time.

'I was in it and I was preaching it. God was doing marvellous things – saving souls,' he remembers. 'I didn't know anything about the Gifts of the Spirit; *not for today* in my Brethren background.'

On the first morning of the campaign, Wally was leading the prayer meeting when he heard someone speaking in tongues. He looked round and saw a little Welsh woman in the corner. She was really an Apostolic Church member, but the Apostolic Church was miles away, so she attended the Holiness Church. Wally was worried. What was he going to do about this?

'A woman!' he thought, 'I'd been brought up Brethren! Speaking in Tongues! I knew that wasn't for today. I'd been taught that! I knew it all. You had to have an interpreter present. I'd been doing some illicit reading in 1 Corinthians 12 and 14. Well, I was critical, but I could hear that it wasn't the babble I'd been led to believe it was.' Wally had to lead the prayer meeting again the next day. He described it:

'God came – Oh, it was a wonderful time. Somebody was crying out to Jesus here. Somebody was a backslider, so-called, and asked for restoration. God was there and I forgot about everything else.' The lady began to speak in tongues again very loudly.

'Now, I've got it,' Wally thought. 'A – it's a woman. B – there's no interpreter present. I've got to stop it.' But, before I did, I said, "Lord, tell us what that means." I'd just said the S of *means* and I was speaking. I can remember, to this day, parts of what came out of my mouth, and I've seen it fulfilled since. It came out of my own mouth!' After the meeting, Wally's fellow campaigner came up to him and said,

'Brother North, I didn't know you had the gift of interpretation.'

'If that's what it is, neither did I!' Years later, when G.W. came across the Pentecostal doctrine of Initial Evidence, he knew from his own experience that it couldn't be right. He had already been baptised in the Holy Spirit, and now he was interpreting, without ever having spoken in tongues himself.

The next day Dolly was due to come over to a campaign meeting. 'I'd got to explain to her,' Wally said. 'She came into the meeting. Sure enough, Mrs. Bolden spoke in tongues. Out came the interpretation through me. My wife was convinced. At least, she knew her husband wouldn't fool about. She was convinced of the truth of it.' On the Sunday it was Wally's turn to lead the meeting. His fellow campaigner, who was going to preach, said to him,

'If the glory comes, brother North, don't bother about me.'

'It was a good job he did', said Wally. 'We were all down on our knees on the platform and everything was happening, but this time I was speaking out and there had not been any message in tongues in front of it. I was speaking out in the same manner.' When it was all over, Mr. Stillwell, the other campaigner, said to G.W,

'I didn't know you had the gift of Prophecy, brother North.'

'Well, if that's what it is, neither did I!'

'That's how green I was. Wasn't God good to me?' was G.W.'s comment on these experiences.

At Auchenheath, G.W. told how, as well as learning about the Gifts of the Spirit from his own experience, he also began to learn about healing in the same way. He admitted,

'I didn't know anything about demons or casting things out when I went to this particular home in the heart of the country. I found that your reputation goes a little bit before you, and, when I got there they'd got a couple of people in this room who had had slipped discs for about six months. One of them was my brother-in-law. They were both in great agony and God healed them. The discs went in like that! God was really working.

We'd had a tremendous prayer-meeting. God had come and filled my brother-in-law. He'd entered into a new realm altogether. The daughter of the house came in and knelt just inside the door. I went over to her, knelt down beside her, and said,

"I'm ever so sorry, love, the meeting's over." All of a sudden, she started to shake and tremble. I couldn't understand this. Whatever was happening? Demons were coming out of her. I was in a new world. I never said, "Come out!" I never said, "In Jesus' name!" I never said anything you're supposed to say. People get up and chant, "In Jesus' name, In Jesus' Name!" I didn't know anything about that. They all fled. God cleared her. You see how I learned these things.'

Back home in Loose, the people knew that their pastor's ministry had changed. The Witness Team would gather every Monday evening to practise singing and to pray.

'What precious times they were,' recalls Anita. 'On one such occasion, Mr. North had been praying and his voice changed from one of praying to one of authority and we knew something had happened. We knew he had spoken in prophecy for the first time. Afterwards he sometimes prayed for one and another who were sick. These were all new experiences for us – very exciting and precious. Some of the team began to experience the Holy Spirit with them in this new way and spoke in tongues.

The team were taken to a Pentecostal church at Ash, near Wrotham, and found it was wonderful to hear more of this teaching, I remember the feeling of awe when we were invited to go with Mr. North and the Pastor to pray for the Pastor's wife. They anointed her with oil!'

Some of the original church members, not agreeing with the turn his preaching had taken, left the church in the latter years of G.W.'s ministry in Loose. But it was G.W.'s links with the Calvary Holiness Church which led to his being called to the pastorate of the C.H.C. in Bradford.

CHAPTER 4
A PREACHER ON FIRE

The campaigners at Gillingham C.H.C. had, after their successful efforts there, recommended Wally North to their denomination as a possible candidate for their vacant Bradford pastorate. Though Wally knew that God was calling him to Bradford, Dolly was not too keen on moving from a lovely village in Kent with an orchard at the bottom of the garden to a Northern city terraced house with a sooty back yard. It was like going to another world. But one day, when she was lying in bed, suffering from a cold, she felt that the Lord gave her the verse, *Arise, shine, for the light has come.* So she arose and went.

For their part, the handful of people at the Bradford C.H.C. had been praying for about nine months for a new pastor. Their previous pastor had been ill and forced to give up the ministry and, though they had been supplied with preachers, often including the leader of the denomination, Rev. Maynard James, they wanted their own pastor, 'to settle down with; someone who could guide us, teach us and organise us. We didn't realise what a culture shock it was going to be!' remembers one of the congregation.

G.W. always claimed that his subsequent ministry was the result of an, 'Outpouring of the Spirit of the Lord' in Bradford.

'I did not begin it,' he confessed. 'I did not take revival. I am a result of it.' He admitted that he 'fiddled about, putting out what are politely called fleeces' for about three to six months after God had told him to go. 'I ought not to have done,' he confessed. 'God expected me to obey Him.'

Bradford was a dirty industrial city in 1952. Before smoke free areas were introduced the buildings were all blackened by the output from the woollen mill chimneys. Situated as it is, surrounded by hills, the city was often under a smoky cloud which would turn into smog on foggy winter days. For Wally, this was a reminder of London fogs.

To Dolly's dismay, the washing was often covered with black specks. She had only a tiny kitchenette and a cellar in which to do the washing – by hand, or with a boiler and mangle. The clothes had to be carried up the outside cellar steps to be hung out to dry. Dolly never complained. Many of the congregation were experiencing the same hardships. Indeed, some of them lived in 'back to back' houses, common in Yorkshire at the time, with outside toilets and tiny patches of garden or yards. The church manse provided better facilities than these.

The terraced, three storey house in St. Leonards Road had four bedrooms and was large enough to accommodate the family, which now included Wally's mother. Her husband having recently passed away, Wally took her to live in Bradford with his family. His father had succumbed to a bout of pneumonia, from which he ought not to have died, his son asserted. The doctor, an alcoholic, had mis-prescribed his father's medicine, with the result that his temperature had been plunged far too low. Some said the family should have protested, but they decided not to make a fuss. After all, Dad was with the Lord and nothing was going to bring him back.

THE CHURCH IN 1952

The Calvary Holiness Church was a denomination founded on Wesleyan teachings by a group of four men – Jack Ford, Maynard James, Leonard Ravenhill and Clifford Filer. They were Cliff College students, who, after going out 'Gospel trekking' together, eventually formed the C.H.C. About forty of these churches came into being, mainly around Lancashire, Yorkshire and Derbyshire. The C.H.C. Bible College was at Stalybridge in Cheshire and, during his earlier days as pastor, Wally travelled there weeky to lecture.

The congregation of Bradford C.H.C. met in a set of rented rooms above a tyre shop on a busy main road at Westgate in the city centre – a far cry from the stone-built village church in a picturesque Kent valley. This building being about thirty minutes walk from the manse, the family often walked three times on a Sunday, though they lived on the most frequent trolley bus route in the city – every three minutes at peak times. Their route lay through factory lined streets and was far from picturesque. For speed, the bus was always taken home. Not many people owned cars in those days.

Wally had not been at the church for very long when he discovered that it was in debt. A church member recalls that he stood up at one meeting and announced 'with a funereal face,'

'My dear wife and I have decided that we're not taking any money from the church until the debt is paid.' It was paid in a very short time. No collecting bags or plates were taken round during meetings. Wally believed that with the blessing of God would come generosity of heart . And so it proved to be. In those early days the pastor was given whatever was left in the offering after all other expenses had been paid. At first this was a very small amount, but, as the congregation grew and people were blessed, the amount in the offerings increased. Then the pastor decided that he wanted to receive a regular salary as he felt he was getting too much!

This decision typified the couple's attitude to money. They were determined not to have many possessions. They stuck to this principle all their lives, even when times were more prosperous. Whatever was not needed for their personal or travelling expenses was given away. Very little remained in their bank account; God would provide for them. They had never been used to having much to spare. Their daughter Marian remembers how, when living in Loose, she came home from school one day, opened the cupboard door and saw nothing there but a jar of jam. She told her mother they had had burglars, but was informed that the food had not been stolen; it had just all been eaten. But God did provide when someone came round with a box of groceries for the hungry family.

On another occasion Dolly was expecting visitors for tea. She had got it into her head that it was rather nice to offer sugar lumps to your guests; but she couldn't afford to buy them. To her surprise and delight, she discovered that someone had left a box of the very commodities she had wished for on the doorstep. She never did find out who had left them there.

A NEW TESTAMENT CHURCH?

G. W. told the people at Auchenheath that before he left Kent to go north he had come to the conclusion that he would not rest until he saw a New Testament church in being. He recognised that the church in Kent of which he had been the pastor had not been a New Testament church.

'That's not a criticism,' he said. 'I was the pastor of the church; you could say it was my fault. I knew it was not a New Testament church because I read of it in the Acts of the Apostles and the church was not like that, nor wanted to be. I knew what I wanted. The only standard of a true church and true church worship must be the New Testament.' Wally went to Bradford determined to be true to what he believed God had put into his heart. He was thankful to God for the smallness of the congregation, seeing it as an advantage not having lots of people to deal with. 'God had mercy on me,' is how he put it. 'I had no plan. I was not seeking revival. Somehow, a great desire to pray came upon me. It was from Heaven itself.'

Although, looking back, G.W. persistently asserted that he had not been seeking a revival, he admitted that he avidly read everything to do with outpourings of the Spirit. His reading included works by Finney, Jonathon Goforth and Campbell Morgan. He well remembered what Finney had said about rules and conditions for revival.

A visit to the North's home and the Bradford church by Duncan Campbell of the Lewis revival was an outstanding event early in Wally's ministry. It was wonderful to hear about his experiences of the power of God and it was not long before the desire for prayer, both of pastor and people, was put into practice.

WAIT ON THE LORD

'From the outset,' relates a church member, 'it was very clear that here was a man of God, well versed in the Scriptures, whose delight it was to share with his new enlarged family the treasures of the Word of God. He himself had entered into an experience of the fullness of the Spirit in his own life and he could not rest until we too were made aware of the great things God had for us – and, indeed, until we had entered in to this new life in the Spirit. But Wally North was not only a man of the Word; he was a man of prayer. We soon became aware that most of our pastor's mornings were spent waiting on God for his flock in the privacy of his bedroom.'

G.W. was always ready to point out that he did not have any of the facilities deemed necessary 'these days' for the carrying out of pastoral duties. Rather he poured scorn on the idea of needing a study or specially designated room. His children remember how, during school holidays, they were always made to keep quiet and not disturb Dad in the mornings. Sometimes they would go upstairs to take him some mid-morning coffee and find him on his knees, wrapped in the eiderdown, with an open Bible on the bed in front of him.

Of course there was no central heating in the house; just a coal fire and back boiler which, in the winter, Dad lit every morning before the children got up. He then got their breakfast whilst Mum was in bed drinking a cup of tea Then the whole family would read a passage from the Bible and Dad would pray before the girls all went off to school. If anyone came to call for the children, they were included in the family prayers. Later, when the girls were teenagers, their father stopped this practice. The girls were becoming too embarrassed in front of their friends.

OUTPOURING

In the 1980s G.W. published two articles in a magazine called the New Covenant Voice. These articles were entitled 'God Came' and 'Outpouring'. In them he described what had happened in Bradford, explaining that the outpouring included the outpouring of the peoples' hearts in prayer as well as the outpouring of the Spirit of God:-

'The favourite text among us [at the church] was very simple: *Wait upon the Lord. Wait, I say, upon the Lord*, or *My soul, wait thou only upon the Lord*. That is exactly what I, and a few others did. Some of them had been praying a long time before I arrived. We prayed constantly almost from the moment I got there. We loved to pour out our hearts together.

I have never heard outpourings of hearts anywhere as I heard in those days. Occasionally I have heard lovely prayers, beautifully phrased, comparable with any you can read out of a book - they had not the power of hearts outpoured. I have heard noisy, shouted prayers too; they have not been the same as the prayer that gripped us in those days. I have heard prayers vibrant with that "something" of the heart; the Spirit of God and the whole spirit of man in it too. I have listened to the whole being of man praying. We used to gather together and pray and go home and pray. We loved it. The real difficulty I had was to stop the people praying; we just prayed and prayed.'

G.W. went on to point out that the notion that a Revival had to cost people everything was proved not to be true in those Bradford days: 'Neither I nor anyone else had a sense of it costing anything. The testimony of all hearts and radiant faces was, "It was a delight, it was a joy; it was indescribable, utterly satisfying and strengthening."

'These people were seeking the outpouring of the Spirit of God,' he said, 'and to get it they poured out their own spirits. They poured out day after day, week after week, month after month, hours upon hours. Surely, before God poured out, as they were seeking Him to, God first poured out on them the spirit of prayer and supplication - all praise be His; but praise to them also that they were big and determined enough to give themselves to such prayer and supplication for so long.'

These were no conventional prayer meetings. G.W. points out that,

'There was never a list for prayer. We weren't praying in tongues particularly. There were no directions - nothing. It became the rule that nobody brought their Bibles either; people who attended were expected to pray - not read the Bible. The general approach was, "They didn't have Bibles on the Day of Pentecost, did they?"

Among that group very few people ever prayed for themselves, or, if they did, it was not for long. When they first came into this tremendous atmosphere of prayer some did ask God to do something for them, but only because they realised they were not in it. Once they got in, that was the end of prayer for self. Free from self, prayers and outpourings abounded for anyone, anything, any situation anywhere.'

One church member describes what happened next:-

'As we prayed our hunger for God intensified, until that glorious Sunday evening when Westgate experienced its own Pentecost, as God poured out His Spirit upon us. We weren't praying for revival. We wanted God to do something for us and in us as individuals, because the pastor had got somewhere that we wanted to get to. The theme of the ministry at that time was Entire Sanctification by the Baptism of the Holy Spirit and fire, resulting in holiness of life.' GW. wrote:

'This was the desire of everyone and the experience of some. Above all else people wanted to be rid of sin; everyone felt that he or she must come right through into what God wanted them to be in Christ. There can be no doubt that this was one of the main reasons for the outpouring.'

THE GLORY CAME

There came a Sunday when the sermon subject for the evening was

Judgement must begin at the house of God.

'That really broke up the congregation,' one member recalls. 'We began to get right with one another, and that was the beginning. Mr. North emphasised that, until we were right with one another, God wouldn't bring them in from the outside. He preached a lot about Holiness and a Clean Heart. Some of us were quite desperate.'

On the Sunday when 'God came' the morning message was 'The glory filling the temple'. GW. recalled that, after the meeting, 'One of our young ladies came to me and said,

"I must have this glory!" G.W., having a mile trek home for lunch and then back again for Bible-class, did not have time to talk or pray with her then, but promised to do so after the evening service. That night, the sermon was on 'Entering into His Rest'. After the service, another young woman, who did not usually go to the meetings, confessed,

'You know, I am not in this that you are talking about.' GW. and another church elder began to talk and pray with the two young people who wanted 'the glory'.

'As we were talking,' said GW. 'I found I had to raise my voice louder and louder – there was quite a noise coming from next door.' In the end, the noise was so loud that GW. had to admit,

"It sounds as though what you want is going on next door. We'd better go!" In the room next door they found fifteen to twenty people 'seeking the glory'. They were on their knees; some radiant with the Glory, others crying out with tears to God. Tears at last turned to cries of joy as one after another stood up, lifting their heads and faces to Heaven; filled with the glory of God.'

NEW BEGINNINGS

'That was the beginning and it continued exactly as it had started,' remembered GW. The congregation soon doubled and then continued to grow. Some of the original members had left, unable to take the new kind of church life. However, the congregation, which had been meeting in 'the small hall' until now, soon had to move into 'the large hall', previously used only for special occasions.

'During these days of change and development,' G.W. wrote, 'preaching for me became as new.' Having never been one who preached from copious notes, he found that 'all the notes were swept away. God came on the preacher as well as the people. He came on everybody; it was absolutely unforgettable. It was beyond anyone's power to shut peoples' mouths. They couldn't stop praying, praising, singing, shouting.'

The Glory had come! To quote Campbell Morgan, 'Divine disorder' reigned in the congregation.

Although physical miracles did take place in those days of blessing, G.W. emphasised that the greatest thing was that 'men and women were transformed. I did not have to mount rescue operations any more. Pastoral visitation went by the board. I was busy dealing with enquiring sinners. All quarrelling stopped dead; no-one seemed to have anything to complain about. Women weren't falling out any more; men saw eye to eye; there was not a frown to be seen. The problem of the caretaking of the church premises was immediately solved - they all volunteered to do it. All internal church problems vanished and stayed that way for years. I never heard a murmur or a complaint. All church decisions were unanimous.'

YOUNG AND OLD ALIKE

The usual attitude for prayer meetings in the Bradford church was that of kneeling. Special rubber kneeling pads were made for use on the hard linoleum floor, broken only by some even more uncomfortable strips of coconut matting. Every Wednesday was a special day for prayer and fasting, beginning at noon and carrying on until the Bible Study began at seven thirty in the evening. Those who were able prayed throughout the half day, with a couple of breaks for cups of tea. Others who had to work would come and join in during lunch hours or after work or school. During school holidays numbers were swollen by teenagers, come to seek God with their elders.

'It's a glorious sight,' G.W. reported in his magazine article, 'to see youngsters mixing with grown-ups, eager to be with them. But that's how it should be. It is when God pours out His Spirit. The Spirit of God was working. Everybody was centred on that; grown-ups and youth; every body seemed to live for that only. One Sunday an old lady of nearly eighty responded to the Lord. The next Sunday it was her grand daughter, nearly eight, who was seeking the blessing. The young people used to be there so much that some of their parents objected and said,

"It's a wonder they don't take their beds down to that place!"

One day a man from the tyre firm next door to the church premises asked if the purpose was to turn the church into a New Testament church. 'What made him ask a question like that?' Wally asked himself. Perhaps he had heard the sound of the people praying and rejoicing, which sometimes made those that were passing by wonder what was going on. They could hear the noise above the sound of the traffic on one of the busiest roads in the city.

One occasion which became very noisy was the day on which a young man was 'set free'. He was a church deacon and his father had been a church elder for many years. During the singing of the Charles Wesley hymn, *And Can it be*, when the verse was reached: *My chains fell off*, his chains fell off and he began to shout, 'Hallelujah! Glory!' at the top of his voice.

Unable to carry on singing the hymn, the rest of the congregation joined in with him. They had not realised that he possessed such a loud voice; he had always been very quiet. He never went back to his former timidity, though he did tone down after a while. Scenes like this were not unusual. It was not all noise, though. Sometimes there were periods of great quietness, when nobody spoke. These were not embarrassed silences, but a great hush seemed to descend on everyone. Some said more was accomplished in those moments than when anyone was preaching.

A Church of England vicar went into the prayer day one Wednesday afternoon. At first he was afraid. He had never in his life heard anyone praying like those people did. He confessed that he didn't know where to go and hide himself; but he was to become a regular prayer with the same people.

In contrast, another man, having seen what was happening in a prayer meeting, challenged GW.:

'What did you come here for?' he said. 'We were alright until you came here.' He fell down on to the floor as he said it. 'Prayer exposed the Devil,' explained GW.

NEEDS WERE MET

During this period never a weekend passed but people were seeking the Lord at the front of the congregation.

'Souls were met in their needs, bodies were healed, devils were cast out; all sorts of things happened; things that ought to happen in church regularly, as the norm,' said GW. Sometimes people used to call out for mercy or Salvation whilst the sermon was in progress. Some even fell off their chairs. One of the church elders, Walter Fisher, an elderly Yorkshire man, used to shout so loudly when he prayed, 'the wicked used to tremble!'

The pastor's Sunday evening sermons were never less than an hour long. 'If it was 45 minutes we thought there was something wrong,' recalls one lady. 'Sometimes, when he stopped preaching you could hear a pin drop – nobody moved. He pronounced the benediction and everybody would sit there, feeling unable to stir for minutes on end.' His daughter Judith can still remember the terror she felt on one occasion when her father had been talking about the madness of King Nebuchadnezzar. His vivid description of the proud ruler's insanity was enough to frighten any who might be so foolish as to resist the sovereignty of God.

PREACHING

G.W. testified that the Holy Spirit was moving in him 'mightily' in those days, revealing truth and opening the Scriptures in an unprecedented way in his life.

'Much came by way of prophecy,' he said. 'That is, following a period of waiting on God, sometimes in private and sometimes in public, I would commence speaking out things I had never known until I spoke them. These things were quite new to me. I taught myself out of my own mouth, and thereby learned the first use of prophecy.'

Ever since his own Spirit baptism experience in Kent, G.W. had been teaching the truth, as he saw it, of Second Blessing Sanctification. i.e.: a person is Born Again, and then needs a second major experience to bring him or her into a life of holiness in the fullness of the Spirit. He began to question this teaching when, as he said, 'The Lord taught me by revelation that the Lord Jesus' birth was a type of our New Birth; that, as in the natural, so in the spiritual, there is ante-natal life – or *quickenings* of the Spirit. These *quickenings* may be, perhaps often are, mistaken for the Birth, but are really just the promises of it.'

During this time of revelation, a question came into G.W.'s mind, relating to the teaching of Entire Sanctification and the Clean Heart as a so-called second Work of Grace:

'I had never thought of it until then. When it came, it was revolutionary to me,' he recalled. 'Can a clean thing come from an unclean?' and the related question, 'Can an unclean thing come from a clean?' were the rhetorical questions in his mind. 'I saw vividly,' he said, 'that a person could not be born of a clean and holy God and yet have an unclean heart and be an unholy person. In a flash it seemed that the whole basis of Second Blessing Holiness crumbled away and, with it, my former beliefs I had for so long been preaching. Perhaps, having never gone through the Holiness school, I had never been an orthodox Holiness preacher anyhow; but I could no longer preach the way I had been preaching, for I immediately saw it to be Scripturally unfounded.'

So, the Holiness teachers' contention that when a person is born of God and becomes regenerate, he is a sinner still, has an unclean heart and is still unholy, GW. now saw as an insult to God, 'though certainly never intended as such,' he conceded. From this point on, he began to preach the reception of and baptism in the Holy Spirit as indistinct from New Birth and to look back on the time of his own experience of the baptism in the Spirit as the time when he was Born Again.

'Nothing is greater than that a man should be born of God and become His son,' he asserted.

INFLUENCES ON TEACHING

Although GW. described his experiences as revelation from God, it may be said that he was influenced by his reading of certain authors, though he claimed that he was not in the habit of reading many books other than the Bible. He certainly did not own shelves full of books.

Shortly after his move to Bradford, his elder, Walter Fisher, gave him his copy of a book entitled, 'Letters of a man of God' [1879], written by an anonymous correspondent. Walter Fisher had been a miner and had known the great Smith Wigglesworth. Wigglesworth, known as 'the Apostle of Faith' was one of the pioneers of the Pentecostal revival at the beginning of the 20th century. G.W. once said that meeting Walter Fisher was crucial to his spiritual development. 'Letters of a man of God' gave him clear insights into Quaker spirituality and led him to read the journal of the founder of Quakerism, George Fox. He often quoted George Fox in his sermons.

G.W. also loved to read the great Holiness teachers, including, above all, Wesley's journals and other writings and sermons. Another much-read teacher was Oswald Chambers, whose direct and uncompromising style was well-loved in the Bradford church. But 'the truth of the New Covenant in Christ' came as a great revelation to GW. and, being convinced that many, if not most Christian churches were still living in the Old Covenant, he preached, often, he felt, as a lone voice, what he saw to be the truth.

Not only did G.W. claim to have had truth revealed to him, but he insisted that his hearers should also have the truths of Scripture revealed personally to them by the Holy Spirit.

'It comes by revelation,' he would say.

Whether his insights into what the Bible teaches were unique at the time and merely backed up by what he read or whether they had in fact stemmed in part from what he had read may be arguable. His testimony was clear that he had received the truths he taught directly from the Lord. He may well have found encouragement in the things he was reading; but the fact that his preaching and teaching was transformed from that time on is beyond dispute and led eventually to a parting of the ways with the Holiness movement.

INDEPENDENCE

Although G. W. North has been called 'a uniquely independent person', the independence of Bradford C.H.C. came about because of disagreements within the denomination. At that time G.W. was producing articles for 'The Flame', a magazine issued by the Holiness movement, still in circulation today. In these articles he began to give accounts of the things which were happening in his own home church. These things included manifestations of the Gifts of the Spirit, which, although not emphasised by G.W., were not encouraged by leaders of the denomination.

The C.H. C. held a yearly Easter Convention at Oldham, just over the Pennines in Lancashire. This was attended with great enthusiasm by most of the Bradford church members, a coach being hired for the occasion. On the Easter Monday following the first 'Outpouring' their pastor was to preach at the Oldham Convention. His subject was 'The New Birth'. Though the Bradford people were delighted at this, their pastor's sermon was coolly received by the proponents of Second Blessing teaching.

Following the sermon, some of the newly blessed people from Yorkshire became a little noisy during the closing prayer and were asked by the leader of the meeting to conduct themselves with more decorum whilst he pronounced the benediction. How could they keep quiet? They were so excited by what was happening to them.

Soon after these events there came a point in 1954 when the leaders of the C.H.C. took the decision to merge with the Church of the Nazarene, an American denomination. There were three major Holiness movements at this time – C.H.C., the International Holiness Mission and the Church of the Nazarene. The latter tended, in those days, to be rather strict in its rules about behaviour, setting out instructions on daily conduct, including rulings on dress, mixing with the opposite sex etc. which were quite daunting.

The negotiations for the merger of the two denominations were going through, but there were several churches which decided against signing up, Bradford being one of them. Perhaps they did not relish the idea of being governed from America. Besides this, G.W.'s departure from conventional Holiness teaching and the Bradford church's freedom to move in the Gifts were not acceptable to the leading ministers. Maynard James, the C.H.C. president, had written to the superintendent of the Church of the Nazarene in Britain asking for freedom of conscience in the matter of 'tongues'. The C.H.C. position with regard to this Gift was that, though it was not to be encouraged, it was not to be forbidden. This, they felt, was in line with Paul's teaching in the Corinthian letter.

However, one young C.H.C. pastor's experience seems to belie this. He met GW. at the ministerial circuit meetings and remembers that he 'stood out. He was unique.' As was their custom, the two ministers exchanged pulpits, and one weekend the young minister was prayed for at the Bradford church and began to speak in tongues. Because of this, he says, he had to leave the C.H.C. Not knowing what to do, having been made homeless as well as jobless, he was taken in by the North family and he stayed on in Bradford, becoming part of the church there. His ministry was much appreciated in their meetings.

Of course, by the time of the merger, the Bradford church was large enough to exist independently, but the decision to separate themselves was not taken lightly. For some of the original members it was sad to leave other members of their denomination, and the pastor visited every person individually to make sure that everyone was with him in the bold step they were about to take. The decision had to be unanimous, he knew, or the church would not prosper. It was always his practice not to make any church decisions without the backing of every member. No-one's opinion was discounted.

The name chosen for the newly-formed church, 'The New Covenant Fellowship', demonstrated the way in which the members intended to live. Their pastor had communicated to them his desire for a New Testament church. One of the church members, who was a sign writer, emblazoned the new name in huge letters on the front of the building. No-one passing the church could have missed it. A special communion service was held in which all the people committed themselves to each other for the future. These were memorable days indeed.

All this did not mean that the church never had anything more to do with people from Holiness denominations. Indeed, young ministers from various Holiness churches, including some from Emmanuel Missions, would come over to Bradford to talk over the great doctrines of the faith with GW. A couple of ex C.H.C. pastors moved over to Bradford to get into the blessing which they found there. GW. and the Bradford church maintained their affinity with the great Holiness teachings on the Clean Heart and the pastor continued to preach on the great Wesleyan doctrines, learned from the Holiness preachers.

DRAWING POWER

Of course Wally and Dolly had kept in touch with friends from Loose Baptist Church. Some of them began to visit Bradford, much to the surprise of other people in the south, who wondered why anyone would want to go there for a holiday. At that time, many of their friends from Kent were not aware of the beauty of the moors and dales close to Bradford's industry. They could think only of dirty woollen mills. But Wally and Dolly would take their visitors for trips and hikes into the dales so that they were able to enjoy the wonderful Yorkshire scenery as well as the blessings in the church..

The house was often full of people, squashed in all over the place, who had heard about the wonderful *times of refreshing* experienced in Bradford, and felt a longing to be part of it. Dolly had to work very hard in her tiny kitchenette. She was never heard to complain of feeling tired.

Perhaps that was because, like everyone else, she felt carried along by the blessing.

Every Sunday the house was full of people for lunch, tea and after-church supper. People had to travel by bus in those days and some of them, travelling a distance, could not be expected to go home between every meeting. Dolly tirelessly catered for many of them. Eventually, Wally's sister Rene and brother-in-law Alf, with their large family, moved up to Bradford from Kent. They 'just wanted God,' Alf said. Rene helped take some of the load from Dolly; the young people now had another home in which to gather on Sundays. Some of them went to Alf for his wise counsel and he soon became an elder in the church. Young people from Kent were to follow, joined by more from different places, seeking to be included in the life of the Bradford congregation.

PENTECOSTAL?

As well as leaving the preaching of accepted Holiness doctrine, G.W. could not agree with the, then widely accepted, Pentecostal teaching. This similarly proclaimed 'The Baptism' as a later, second great work of the Spirit, following the New Birth.

After the split from the Holiness movement, New Covenant Fellowship people began to go to an Easter Convention at a local Bradford Pentecostal church, known as Dean House. Cecil Cousen was the minister of this flourishing church. Though differing in outlook, he and Wally became friends, often working together. Indeed, the young people's choir from N.C.F., trained and conducted by their pastor, used to sing at the Dean House convention. They loved going to Dean House and the people there seemed to love their singing. Cecil Cousen was to publish several articles by GW. North in the Voice of Faith magazine, bringing him into contact with leading ministers of the time.

Many of the Pentecostal people were taught that the Baptism in the Spirit had to be accompanied by 'Speaking in Tongues' and, indeed, this phenomenon was widely called the 'Initial Evidence' of being filled with the Spirit. This had not been Wally's own experience. He had interpreted, prophesied and used the Gift of Healing before he had spoken in Tongues. Moreover, he found that 'Initial Evidence' was not recorded in Scripture as being true for everyone, so could not be taught as universally the case. More importantly, he found that, regrettably, some people were trying to force themselves to speak with Tongues, in order to be accepted as genuinely Spirit-filled. This resulted in spurious experiences and much heart-ache. To quote:

'The psychological effect and spiritual impact of such claims on untaught souls has been to lay them open for pseudo-baptisms, and, in some cases, wrong possession. Perhaps the degree of confusion it creates is one of the worst features of the theory.'

He further observed, 'That the gift in operation during or following Baptism in the Spirit is generally Tongues is without controversy, but sometimes other Spiritual Gifts operate before Tongues. Sometimes, in fact, many times, no supernatural demonstrations accompany the experience at all.'

'In the end,' he maintained, 'it is the fruit of the Spirit as recorded in Galatians five that is the proof or evidence of the fact that a person has been baptized in the Spirit and is living and walking in the Spirit.'

Perhaps, following the widespread Charismatic movement of the second half of the last century, the topic of 'Initial Evidence' may not be so important an issue for discussion amongst Christians. However, it remained topical enough for GW. to publish a paper on the subject in 1976, revised and re-issued in 1980, from which the above quotations are taken.

MIRACLES IN BRADFORD

At the beginning of G.W.'s own testimony, 'What makes a man tick', he said that he had never claimed to possess the Gift of Healing or the Gift of Miracles.

'As a matter of fact, I don't think I have any of the Gifts,' he said.

'What I know,' he continued, 'is that, at some time or another, I have seen all the Gifts in operation.'-'Through me,' he may have added, for that is what he meant. He added that he had always found that God had performed miracles as signs. Some people had the ability to perform a remarkable healing as a testimony to the truth of the Gospel they were preaching, though this may not be their particular ministry. He classed himself in that category. To illustrate this he related two stories of outstanding healings which had taken place during his ministry in Bradford.

SPINA BIFIDA

Lily was a young woman in a 'dreadful state'. She had tried to commit suicide when on holiday, and was 'saved by my wife's prayers,' said G.W.. Dolly had been on her knees in the caravan, praying for Lily, who had run away from them. 'She got caught on the rope of a buoy and God saved her life,' GW. related. 'One day Lily was delivered from all her demons, so that she said she felt like dancing for joy.'

But Lily was under a Psychiatric Social Worker, who didn't approve of G.W.'s 'swinging her on to religion', and had organised another kind of dance for the following Friday. This was arranged to help with the rehabilitation of people suffering from depression and other psychiatric illnesses. Now Lily did not want to go; now she didn't need to be cheered up; but GW. told her to carry on as usual. 'There'll be someone there you can talk to about Jesus,' he said. Little did he know what was to follow.

Sure enough, as Lily was sitting out the dances, feeling like a wallflower, a lady sat beside her and asked why she wasn't dancing. So Lily told her what Jesus had done for her.

'Do you think Jesus would do anything for my Angela?'

'Yes; look what He's done for me.'

The following Saturday, Lily returned to the church and reported the happenings to the pastor.

'Who's Angela, Lily?'

'She's her baby. She's ill. She's never moved since the day she was born. She's just alive. She's got something wrong with her spine.'

When Wally heard this, his heart sank. His sister Rene had had a baby with Spina Bifida. She had died at the age of nine months. When baby Sandra died the doctor had said to his sister, 'You'll be an angel when you get to Heaven,' for nursing the baby and keeping her alive for so long.

Not knowing what he was going to do, Wally told Lily to tell Angela's mother to come to the church on Sunday and bring the child. He had seen God deliver many people, but this was a completely new realm for him. Of course he was hoping that the mother would come to the evening service and hear the Gospel preached. She didn't come. Then, just as the pastor had pronounced the benediction, the door opened and in walked the mother, carrying the child.

'On her arm she had a large white pillow and on the pillow lay the child. You couldn't touch it. It hadn't moved since it was born,' is how G.W. described the scene. Lily went down and brought the mother and baby to the front of the hall. GW. felt his heart sink again. What could he do?

'Oh, God, heal this child,' was all he could say. That was it. The mother and child went home.

Within a week the child was beginning to pull herself up in her cot. At the monthly clinic the doctors asked,

'What has happened to this child?' The mother told them. They were sceptical. At the end of the following month the child walked into the clinic behind her mother. Then the doctors had to admit:

'It's a miracle!'

'I saw God do it. I didn't do anything,' was G.W.'s confession. 'The mother never became converted. She just came along to church for a few more weeks. Miracles don't save peoples' souls. The last time I saw the child she was out shopping in the city with her mother. God healed her.'

MR. MYCOCK

Mr. Mycock was a long standing member of the Queensbury Calvary Holiness Church, near Bradford. Cecil Cousen, of Dean House, was a friend of Willie Mycock's, and one day Cecil dropped in to inform Wally that Willie was dying.

'If you want to see Willie alive,' he said, 'you'd better go now. His waterworks have collapsed. He's in a coma. His wife's there. I'm going to see him now. If you want to see him alive in this world, go up now.'

After delivering this sad news Cecil left for the hospital, thinking that Wally would soon be following him. However, though his wife repeatedly reminded him that he ought to be keeping his word to go and see the sick man, Wally could not bring himself to do so.

'Love, I can't go and see him,' he explained, when it got to teatime. 'I don't know what's the matter. I can't go and see him.'

"I couldn't get up and put a coat on to go," G.W. remembered. The next day came and Willie was still alive. It was the same story. Though reminded again by his wife, and willing to keep his word, "I couldn't go and see him," said GW. The next day was Wednesday, the day of fasting and prayer. Wally remembered feeling embarrassed at the thought of facing the people at the meeting:

"I'd got to face all my fasters and prayers, who all knew about Willie, and confess I'd not been to see this wonderful old man of God. You should have seen their faces. They couldn't understand this; I couldn't understand it myself. This went on for exactly a week. I had to face them over Sunday. I expect they thought I'd lost any love I'd ever had, or any concern for anybody."

Exactly a week after Cecil Cousen's visit Wally was sitting indoors. He suddenly felt he had to visit the hospital, picked up his coat and went up the hill to Bradford Royal Infirmary, where Willie still lay. On going into the hospital, Wally met a nurse, filling hot water bottles, who told him,

'We're just trying to make him comfortable. If you wait a minute you can go in and see him.'

What happened next was a lesson to Wally on the timing of God. For the first time since the coma began Willie Mycock opened his eyes as his visitor entered the room. The patient was not a pretty sight. He was propped up in bed with tubes all over him and a cradle over his body to keep the covers away from him. Wally didn't recognise him because his face was covered with large sores.

"The bed was rattling," he recalled. "I walked round the bed and put my arm around him. He sat up. I said,

'Jesus!' I don't know what happened. Something in me erupted." The bed stopped rattling. After that, Wally kept repeating, 'Jesus!' until Willie joined in, feebly at first. The words changed to, 'Victory! Hallelujah!'

"God had healed him," G.W. explained. "I never said anything else. There are no formulae. There's nothing to say. There's every thing to do. It's to love them."

'Where am I? How did I get here?' Willie wanted to know. He couldn't remember being taken to hospital and didn't know his wife had been at his bedside. The doctor came to see what was going on. Being a Catholic, he told Willie, 'You've been to the Pearly Gates, but Peter wouldn't let you in.' The nurse who arrived to clean up the patient's skin confessed,

'You're the first man I've ever nursed who got better from gangrene.'

"I didn't get a word out of the blue," G.W. said, telling this story. "I went to see him when I felt I could. I suddenly felt released." Willie lived to go and join the Bradford congregation in their days of fasting and prayer.

BROKEN LEG

Another quite remarkable healing, recounted by a church member, took place at the pastor's home one holiday afternoon. A group of church people were having tea when a local mother carried her son round to the house. He'd been playing football in the street and there'd been an accident.

'His leg was out here; the bone was all jagged,' described one observer. 'The pastor just prayed with him and it went back. I can hear the scrunch now! And he walked home.' The leg remained whole and football playing continued.

Passing into God

At the end of his testimony sermon at Auchenheath, GW. laid stress on the importance of fasting and prayer; particularly prayer, in explaining what made him 'tick'. He placed great importance on his personal 'waiting on God' and on the many hours spent in the same manner with his congregation. He would often go down to the church before anyone else arrived and walk up and down the aisles praying or lie on the coconut matting 'getting into God' as he called it.

'If you think there's any other way, you have no hope whatsoever of it [the outpouring of the Spirit]. It rests upon passing into God. It's a matter of getting your priorities right. It's only a matter of coming into line with eternal principles which cannot be moved and from which God will never vary. There's nothing deep about this. Wait on God and God comes,' was the message to those gathered, wanting to know what had made this preacher into the person they were listening to in 1975. The fact that churches were built from his ministry, GW. put down to these days of 'waiting on God', particularly in Bradford. Though others have referred to events there as 'Renewal' or 'Revival' he did not himself use these accepted Christian terms.

GW. described the 'outpouring' as coming in three waves, occurring over a period of time, with lulls, as it were, in between. Indeed, throughout the whole of his thirteen years in Bradford, people would become concerned if the 'blessing' seemed to be receding. They had become so used to the moving of the Spirit, that if they felt the movement was waning, they would call extra days and nights of prayer at weekends to get themselves back on track. Nothing but the fullness of blessing was acceptable to them, though others would have called theirs a thriving church. It seems people arranged their lives around spiritual matters.

A HECTIC PROGRAMME

The constant prayer was not, G.W. emphasised, an excuse for not being busy in other ways. He believed in having a packed church programme, because, he reasoned, if people were not busy in the Lord's work, worldly pursuits would soon take its place. Slacking did not come into his mind, for himself or anyone else.

The main morning and evening Sunday services were preceded by half an hour of prayer. Sunday School and adult Bible class were held in the afternoon. Children from nearby blocks of flats were collected up and brought to Sunday school, some of them by bus. In due course, an after-church outreach meeting for young people was started. The church young people went out into the town inviting other young people in for refreshments and to join in a Gospel youth meeting.

Tuesday was the night for the youth meeting, run by the pastor. In this, following his own pastor's example, he tried to train the young people to speak publicly from an early age, giving them subjects on which to give a talk. Wednesday was prayer and fasting day, beginning at noon, followed by an evening Bible exposition; Thursday was the prayer meeting night; Friday was a night off and Saturday involved an open-air meeting in the town centre, preceded by prayer and followed by a Prayer, Praise and Testimony meeting in the evening. This was followed, after some years, by a Late Night Meeting, which involved going out into the city and bringing people, sometimes the worse for drink, into the church for a cup of coffee and a dose of the Gospel. This finished at about 1am. and was not usually attended by the pastor; he had to be fresh for the next day.

Dolly could sometimes be heard to remark that she thought there were too many meetings, and that people should learn to live together at home; her husband could be heard to remark that, in general, people were ' too slack, too lackadaisical and too bone idle lazy to give themselves over to the main thing – waiting on God.'

Of course, apart from at least three sermons or Bible expositions a week, there was all the usual pastoral work of visitation and helping people in more practical ways, such as decorating houses. All this was without the help of a car. Wally did own a bicycle, but found that the hills of Bradford were much more difficult than the lanes of Kent, so the bike was soon abandoned. Fortunately the bus service was good and many miles were walked.

BIBLE TEACHING

'Normal' church life went on throughout those years of particular blessing. It wasn't all prayer. Wally laid a lot of emphasis on Bible teaching; every Wednesday evening he opened up aspects of the Old and New Testaments to a growing group of listeners. Amongst these, the studies in the lives of Abraham and Moses were outstanding. The studies on Abraham proved so popular that in the weeks before he left Bradford, on request, G.W. repeated them every night for some weeks. Another subject well-remembered dealt with all aspects of 'The Church'. These included: the Church and Membership; Worship; the Gifts of the Spirit; Holiness; Government; Money; War; Sin; Fruitfulness; the Law; Prayer; Guidance; Service.

'The Bible studies were something else,' one church member recalls. In fact, they became so well known in the district that people from other churches began to attend and soon these meetings had to be held in the Large Hall. A single subject often took many months to study. For instance, 'The Church' studies went on for over a year and those on Abraham for five months. These were the days before the introduction of tape recorders or cassettes, so a young lady in the congregation, a secretary, would take down the Bible studies in shorthand and produce notes for further reference. This church was certainly not lacking in knowledge of the Scriptures. Their pastor was seeking to pass on to his congregation the same benefits that he had experienced under his old pastor in Plaxtol.

The main preaching service in those days was on Sunday evening, when the pastor would preach for around an hour at the Gospel Service. This was the best attended service of the week and he would be speaking to a packed congregation. The preacher made an impressive figure striding up and down the large platform, waving his arms around for emphasis and sometimes shouting at the top of his voice.

People were known to complain if it got too loud. He was often the subject of skits at Christmas parties, when the actors would imitate his style and his habit of disappearing into the vestry in the middle of his sermons to remove his waistcoat, put his jacket back on and resume preaching. Immaculate dressing for preaching was essential in those days. Dolly took pride in turning out her husband in the whitest shirts with beautifully starched collars, and, although the starched collars disappeared, G.W., throughout his life, always dressed smartly for church meetings.

Sunday mornings were open meetings, given over mainly to worship. And what worship went on in those days! Many visitors would come just to be in that atmosphere of freedom. They enjoyed the worship as much as the preaching. The pastor was not the only one to speak. He wanted to encourage and develop ministries other than his own. He believed it to be part of his pastoral ministry to bring on other preachers. So other men would give messages and the Gifts of the Spirit would be in operation. Usually, time permitting, the pastor would speak for ten or twenty minutes at the end of the meeting, drawing together the strands of all the messages and giving a word of his own. Occasionally there would be no preaching at all because the worship was flowing so freely.

On Saturday evenings everyone was encouraged to give testimonies or short 'words' from the Scripture. There was lots of singing and sometimes there were lots of laughs. If anyone had not been heard for a long time people would ask them, 'When are you going to speak? We haven't heard you for ages.' Everybody was expected to have something to testify about, or a word from their own reading of the Scriptures. There was prayer and worship too. Anything could happen; it was a kind of relaxed meeting in between the open air ministry of the afternoon and the Late Night Meeting of the evening. Again, the pastor would speak to draw this time to a close.

A BARRACK ROOM

Being himself a musician and singer, Wally wanted his congregation to sing 'properly'. Indeed, he would at times stop them in the middle of a verse of a hymn if he thought they weren't making enough effort. 'Open your mouths!' was his cry. They had to get both the tune and the timing right. This would generally, but not exclusively, take place on a Saturday night, when they could have a practice for other meetings. People good naturedly accepted his criticisms and, after practising for a little while, went on with the hymn.

A youth choir, formed by the pastor, would go around singing at various events in the county. He taught them to sing such songs as, *All there is of me, Lord*, and *Let me burn out for thee*. He would not let them get away with anything less than out and out devotion to the Lord and His work, at least in what they sang. This was in line with his description of the Church as 'a barrack room, not a hospital.' Many of the songs sung in the youth meetings in those days were about being good soldiers of Jesus Christ, a sentiment enthusiastically adhered to by this pastor, who had refused to fight for his country. In his Loose days he had drawn a large cross over hymns in the Baptist hymnal, such as *I vow to thee my country* and *O valiant hearts* and had written 'Blasphemy!' in large letters beside them. In time the choir was superseded by a band and singing group, which performed in youth events, though not in the main services.

The congregation were used to the Pastor altering words in hymns which he did not consider to be putting over good doctrine. Some people thought this was nit-picking; but G.W. insisted on people 'singing the truth to themselves'.

HYMNS OF ETERNAL TRUTH

Wesley's hymns were undoubtedly the favourites amongst the Bradfordians. They were sometimes sung over and over again in the meetings, with the result that people would testify to having been greatly blessed and helped into the experience of the hymn writer. So great was G.W.'s desire to have his congregation and others 'singing the truth' that he got together with a local Baptist minister, who had been influenced by his ministry, and had become a visiting preacher at NCF. They, along with others, collaborated to produce a hymn book consisting entirely of poetry by the Wesley brothers. They were set mainly to existing tunes, though G.W. himself was one of several composers of new tunes for these hymns. The new book was called, 'Hymns of Eternal Truth.'

Throughout his life G.W. exhorted his hearers to avoid 'jingles' and get into the, 'sublime as it is Heavenly' poetry of the Wesleys. 'In this realm they have no betters and few, if any, equals,' he wrote in his preface to the music edition of the hymn book.

In common with others, of course, G.W. believed that hearts were crying out for the realities expressed in the writings of the Wesleys, 'born in revival', and coming from 'the Spirit of life then breathing throughout the land'. In those pre-worship group and praise workshop days this pastor wanted his people to be able to join in with the 'heart cries' in the 'language of the Spirit' expressed in these poems. Some people began to refer to the hymns as 'Hymns of Eternal Length', speaking of the added verses from the original poems included in several of them.

Though first conceived of and toiled over in Bradford, 'Hymns of Eternal Truth' was not printed in word form until 1968 and in music form in 1972. Ever since, it has been used, alongside other more well known books for congregational singing in Fellowships and some other churches. It was G.W.'s belief that, 'Our Lord gave them to His church, and wherever souls long for the language of the Spirit, these songs will be sung by all so blessed as to know them.'

It is interesting that in 2007, the principal of the Church of the Nazarene college, when preaching at the annual conference at Rora, revealed that it was his custom to give all his students a copy of 'Hymns of Eternal Truth'. He is now the editor of 'The Flame' magazine, in which G.W. had first written about the 'Outpouring' in the Bradford church. In 2008 he published an article by the same author on 'Forgiveness'. More than forty years had elapsed.

SOCIAL LIFE

If all this sounds rather serious, it is worth recording that G.W. also taught his young people choruses such as, 'The Devil and me, we can't agree' to lighten things up and Sunday evening services always began with chorus sessions, led by various people. Not all of these were deeply theological and the singing of solos and group pieces were regular features of these meetings. The people just loved to have a 'good old sing' without trying to be highly spiritual. After these sessions, the pastor would take over the rest of the service. In later years, leading meetings much larger than those in Bradford was one of his great abilities. He revelled in conducting the singing and worship as well as in the preaching.

'Wally North enjoyed life' is the memory of one of his Northern congregation. 'Bank holiday Mondays saw practically the whole fellowship bundled on to a bus, heading out for the Yorkshire Dales.' Everyone was included, from the youngest to the oldest. Wally found that many of his people, though living amongst such natural beauty, had never explored the Dales. He set out to put that right.

In those days most people had only two weeks annual holiday, including 'Bowling Tide' which was the week when the mills closed down. The working week was usually five and a half days, so Wally thought people needed to get away from their usual environment. Not everything could be cured spiritually; sometimes all people needed was a good day out. Many happy hours were spent hiking, talking and playing games in wonderful surroundings. In summer Wally would take the Youth Fellowship out for walks on long light evenings, replacing their usual meetings.

CHRISTMAS

And Christmas! Christmases were outstanding in the N.C.F. calendar. Beside the Sunday School party, there was a Young Peoples' Party – for under thirties–, as well as a church party. Wally revelled in organising these events, which included lots of hilarious sketches as well as riotous games, especially for the young people.

'Too rough, Dear!' was one of Dolly's comments, which apparently went unheeded.

During the week before Christmas all evening meetings were cancelled so that the pastor could take the young people, and whoever else wanted to go, out carol-singing. This was not for money; but for pure enjoyment. In those pre-car owner days, everyone got on to the bus and travelled to people's homes all over the city. They would sing [properly!] several songs, accompanied by an accordion, and, of course, conducted by the pastor, and then go inside the house for mince pies, home made ginger wine and hot drinks.

The week always ended on Christmas Eve at the manse, for last refreshments before the big Day. On the last Sunday evening before Christmas there was a very unconventional Carol Service. All the old Carols, chosen by the congregation, were sung with gusto and Wally, to the delight of the ladies, used to make all the men crowd up on to the large platform and perform 'God rest ye merry gentlemen,' and 'Good

Christian men.' Then he would call people up to sing a verse of the carol they had chosen. No-one refused. That was the only Sunday in the year when the sermon was only fifteen minutes long!

Boxing Day was a huge day for the family, as the Norths invited anyone in the church who wanted to, to go to their house in the afternoon. People were not asked to bring any food with them, so Dolly was up early, baking for teatime.

'Why do you invite all these people?' asked one of the pastor's daughters.

'Well, dear, some of them don't have a good family Christmas.' And so the small terraced house was crammed with people, as many as thirty, enjoying party games, charades and board games far into the night. The girls loved it. Was Dolly exhausted? She never said so.

FAMILY FEELING

'Number 15' as people called the manse, was an open house to all. Against the advice of other, more prudent people, the door was never locked. Occasionally things were stolen by some shadier visitors, but the attitude was, 'We haven't got anything worth taking,' and it was considered important to have an open door.

Sometimes the girls were shifted out of their bedrooms to make room for needy people to whom their parents were ministering. They never minded this; it was quite normal for them. It made life interesting and varied, even though the behaviour of some of their visitors was rather strange! Their father was only following in his parents' footsteps. A life of sacrifice was called for from disciples of Jesus. This was taken for granted, and every ounce of humour extracted by the girls from many not very funny situations.

His children knew that their interests came second to the interests of the work of God in their father's heart and practice. If the school speech day happened to be on a prayer meeting evening Dad would not be at the school event. It was a bit disappointing, but taken for granted, so not resented. It was made up for when one of the girls reported that her friend's mother, after meeting Dad at a parents' evening, had gone home and exclaimed, 'Isn't Mr. North handsome!' That was worth a lot! Besides, life in the church was exciting and some very interesting people visited their home. They certainly never felt that they had missed out because of their father's profession. There was always something going on; life was never dull.

Something that this pastor did for the male members of his congregation was to give them free haircuts. When his father had become practically blind, Wally had bought a barber's kit to use on his hair, and so had acquired some skill in this direction. Perhaps people were not so fussy in those days, or were more interested in saving money!

Many of Wally's sermons were on the subject of 'Love' and he sought to show the love of God to the people, some of whom, he knew, had never experienced true love in their human families. One of his young people, many years later, recalled that, 'God wrought within our fellowship a wonderful "togetherness" that I, personally, have never experienced since.'

MISSIONARY ZEAL

Having been raised in a Godly home which so practically demonstrated the need for going out to reach the lost, both spiritually and materially, G.W.'s aim throughout his pastoral days, was to preach the Gospel, and to take the church with him in this, though they were already a missionary minded congregation. This was what made him 'tick', as well as preaching Bible truths.

Besides the meetings described earlier, the church did door to door visitation, helped with Billy Graham and T.L.Osborne crusades and held Gospel Campaigns of their own. A branch church was started in a different area of the city. This was pastored by one of the church elders and the people would take it in turns to go and help him on Sundays. They also visited public houses, selling Gospel magazines and singing. They were often mistaken for the Salvation Army, though without any uniforms.

The move of the Spirit had the effect of making them outward looking. On Sunday evenings, after the service, the young people would go out into the city, on their doorstep, and invite other youngsters roaming around the town into the church for free refreshments and to hear the Gospel. Modern 'group' music was used for these events, though not yet in the main services. These meetings resulted in young lives being won over. One of G.W.'s own future sons-in-law was introduced to the Gospel in one of them. His Science teacher, whose life had been transformed, was an elder of the church. The teacher had been invited to speak at the sixth form debating society and had given the students his testimony. Though they had intended to pull his theories to pieces, they were unable to argue with the story he had told them. Intent on putting their opposing points across, several of the sixth-formers decided to go to the Sunday night youth meeting, led by their teacher, and heckle. Instead, they found themselves joining the church.

G.W. quoted the apostle Paul in describing his motivation –*'Woe is unto me if I preach not the Gospel'* – and he would often urge his flock to support foreign missionaries, as well as aiming to 'go out' themselves if possible. One of his young people recalls that her pastor kept his promise to visit her if she got on to the mission field by spending his 65th birthday with her and her family in Ivory Coast .

Having close links with the WEC. Missions, the church invited a missionary speaker once a month instead of the regular Bible studies. Other missions were included in this support and it was considered essential to be 'missionary minded'. Not to be thus minded was inconceivable for NCF. members and they went to many missionary conferences and rallies, giving generous financial support along the way.

It was not the fashion in those days of limited travel to make short term visits to the mission fields, but G.W. was enthusiastic when any of his church members considered sacrificing their comfortable Western lives for a missionary career. In later life he was delighted when one of his daughters went with her husband and family to a missionary life in Africa.

MINISTERS' FRATERNAL

During the last few years of his Bradford pastorate, G.W. joined a group of the city's ministers, known as the Ministers' Fraternal. This group met periodically to discuss, amongst other things, questions of theology. No doubt, G.W. was the only one among them without any formal theological training; but he caused quite a stir when he presented a paper on 'The New Birth', on 1st July, 1957. The points he put down as an introduction to this paper are:-

The New Birth is that sovereign act of God whereby, of Himself, He begets Himself a son.

1. It is intrinsically the supreme revelation of God, wherein the whole powers of the Holy Trinity are engaged.
2. It imparts to the individual the conscious life of God, the life which is in His Son – eternal life.
3. It introduces into the Kingdom of God.
4. It initiates into the New Covenant.
5. It involves the cessation of the old life, this being implemented into the
individual by:

a} Identification with Christ in His death, burial and resurrection.

b} The purification of the heart from all sin.

c} The reception of the Holy Ghost, who is the Spirit of the life that is in Christ Jesus.

This is the logical sequence in any New Birth.

6. It includes {as pre-requisites} conversion, forgiveness, justification and sanctification. {John's New Birth equals Paul's justification and sanctification; which latter are set forth as successive crises by Paul, whereas John nowhere sets forth New Birth as a crisis experience, but assays to prove it by the resultant life}. These various phases of experience can be synchronous, but are often appropriated severally.
7. It is infallibly proven by the indwelling of the Holy Ghost.
8. It incorporates {baptises} into the body of Jesus Christ.
9. It incarnates Christ in the flesh {my body}.
10. It is illustrated by the birth of Jesus Christ.
11. It is ignorantly confused, oftentimes, with lesser manifestations and operation of The Spirit.
12. It is imperative for all believers.
13. It is instantaneous upon true repentance.

He goes on to expand on these points and ends by saying,

'Much more could be said, I know. To finish I would add that the only real proof of the true Birth is the God-nature, love, in us; apart from this nothing is genuine.'

There is no record of the reactions of the assembled ministers to this quite revolutionary {at the time} way of putting theological truth. However, G.W. took on the leadership of this association, so there must have been many points of agreement.

Because, as G.W. always claimed, he did not have time to read many books other than the Bible, with the help of Young's Concordance, he would give books to other people to read and ask them to tell him about the contents, thus keeping himself aware of what was being taught. People were not always convinced by his claims to being uneducated when they heard him quote from various secular and spiritual writings when he preached.

PASTURES NEW

It was in 1963 that events began to move towards G.W.'s moving from Bradford and, consequently, his ministry becoming more widely known. These events began with a lady from Liverpool who was seeking the Baptism in the Spirit. She had actually been to America to be prayed for, so desperate had she been for this experience. She came home to her group in Liverpool to tell them that she had found her travels to be fruitless. This group was from an Anglican church - St Saviour's, Faulkner Square, where the young curate, ex Royal Marine, Rev. Norman Meeten, was leader of a gathering of people who were seeking the Lord.

'Some of us had been baptized in the Spirit,' he recalls.

The lady in question, Joan Porter, was the wife of Dr. Porter, who was the Assistant Supervisor of a Criminal Mental Hospital near Liverpool. Norman Meeten's group would go into the hospital on Wednesdays and Fridays to hold meetings and talk to patients.

Mrs Porter decided to go to her caravan in Wales to fast and pray for God to meet her desires. Nothing happened; so she asked the Lord, 'What do I do now?' She felt that He spoke the words to her, 'In the midst of the battle you will be anointed'. Then she remembered that someone had told her about a church in Bradford that was experiencing the blessing she had been looking for.

One Sunday she got into her car and drove to Bradford. Arriving half an hour late for the service, she opened the door very quietly and, to her astonishment, heard a man half way down the church hall say the words, 'In the midst of the battle you will be anointed.' Then she felt the Spirit of God fall on her and her search had ended.

After the service Mrs Porter invited G.W. to go and speak at one of the hospital meetings in Liverpool. After the meetings the group would go back to the Porters' house to have a meal and a meeting of their own. G.W., realising that the Lord was moving in this group of Anglicans, began to go over to Liverpool on a more regular basis to speak at the hospital and teach the group afterwards. He would often stay on to speak at the Friday meeting too. Norman Meeten became a visiting speaker at the Bradford church. His testimony was that, before he had been baptized in the Spirit, he had called on the Lord 'out of sheer desperation. No-one else was involved.' He had said to the Lord, 'Unless you meet me, I'm finished.'

At the time Norman was chairman of the trustees of The Longcroft, a large house on the Wirral in Cheshire, which had been inherited by a missionary in India. Her mother had had a vision for the house; that it should be a home 'for the setting free of the captives.' This was incorporated into the deeds. The Porters were among the trustees of the house and their idea was that it should be a temporary home for helping those who were mentally, psychologically or emotionally in trouble.

After many months of visiting the group in Liverpool, G.W. was invited to go and take up the position of Spiritual Overseer of the Longcroft. For some time he had been feeling that his time in Bradford was coming to an end. He had begun to realise that he could not be a good pastor and travel too. The Liverpool people had introduced him to a much wider sphere of ministry than he had been formerly accustomed to and he was beginning to be invited to various places to preach.

When Wally communicated his feelings to his church people, however, they urged him to stay. Realising that he had gifts which should be shared with others, they assured him that they would not hinder him in any way. So he hesitated. Norman was not very popular with the Bradford congregation for taking their pastor away, as they saw it.

In the end, as the family was now grown up, and two of the girls had left home, Wally and Dolly felt free to go the way that God seemed to be leading them. It was far from easy for them to leave the place where so much had happened to bind them to their flock. But, having put into place the men he thought would carry on his ministry, G.W., with his wife and their youngest daughter, was sent off to his new life on the Wirral.

'It was an all-embracing ministry,' says one church member of his time in Bradford. 'In 1965, when he moved to The Longcroft, Wally North left a big gap in our fellowship, but he also left us with a wonderful inheritance – twelve years of rich ministry, which had led many of us into a deeper understanding of the things of the Spirit. I suppose, if I were to enumerate the most outstanding lessons which I learnt in those days and which remain just as precious today, they would include:

To know God for oneself; not merely about God.

To come to a place of perfect rest and peace in God.

To be utterly reliant on God at all times and for all things.

It is interesting that before he left Bradford, one of his parishioners remembers that GW. said to her,

'You must pray for me, that the Lord will keep me humble. There's a sense in which I am afraid that I won't be able to deal with the popularity.'

CHAPTER 5
AN INFLUENTIAL PREACHER

THE LONGCROFT AND LIVERPOOL

Wally and Dolly began their new life on the Wirral living in the Lodge on the Longcroft estate in Barnston, a small village near Heswall. With them went their youngest daughter Carole, leaving her friends behind. She soon found a job in Heswall and settled there, her two older sisters remaining in Bradford, feeling slightly abandoned, to continue with their careers.

The contrast between the city terrace and the country bungalow, surrounded by gardens, must have struck home to Wally, almost as much as the contrast between Bethnal Green and Plaxtol so many years ago. God had provided for them richly. They had been willing to leave a country village in Kent for a city street in Bradford and now every thing was clean and picturesque again. A Mini car was bought for Wally's use; but he had not driven since shortly after the war and proved to be rather a madcap driver. The family hated being passengers when Dad was driving and Dolly preferred to go shopping on the bus! To be fair, though, she sometimes refused lifts from other drivers when her husband was away because she wanted the chance to go out on her own and meet other people.

These were times of great change for Dolly. She missed being at the centre of church life, and wondered what she would find to do away from her busy existence in Bradford. There was no church to care for any more and no Fellowship at The Longcroft at that time. But she soon found plenty to occupy her time; as well as looking after the family and other visitors she helped with the cleaning and cooking at the big house.

The family began to attend an Emmanuel [Holiness] church in nearby Pensby on Sunday mornings. They found warm fellowship there. Eventually, Carole's wedding was held at this church, after which The Longcroft put on a wonderful reception for her

Wally, as spiritual overseer, began to minister to the people who came for help to the big house. Many of them were in tremendous need; but some amazing things happened in those early days. One of the people who came to stay was the secretary of the director of a missionary society. She had gone blind and her concerned boss was convinced that this was not for medical reasons; but he didn't know what to do. Having already taken her to all the specialists he knew in London, when he heard of the Longcroft and the ministry there he sent his secretary to see whether anything could be done to help her.

After talking to her, G.W. told her that he wanted her to fast and pray until the next morning, when he would come again to see her. He told her that when he prayed for her, she would be able to see. Next day he duly came into the library and counselled her again. He asked her to repent of the hatred she had in her heart for her abusive father, loving him by faith. Having done that, she knelt down and G.W. laid hands on her and prayed that, in the name of Jesus, the spirit of blindness would be removed. Another person who was in the room remembers vividly,

'I saw the light dawning in her eyes, and then she could see.'

John Norris, who was the Longcroft administrator at the time, talks about how he learned a valuable lesson from working alongside G.W. in those days. One little lady, a primary school teacher, had come to the Longcroft seeking for deliverance from attacks in which she saw a certain symbol. John went off on his scooter to a Liverpool library to look up the meaning of this symbol. When he arrived back and called on GW. to give him the information he had found he was met with,

'Ah, you've found out that it's the Egyptian goddess, Isis.'

'You already knew!'

'Tell me, John, after studying darkness for two hours, how do you feel?'

'Oh, I've got a headache and I feel sick.'

'Learn a lesson, young man. You don't have to study the Devil to defeat the Devil.'

John recalls how, 'faithfully, patiently, time after time, G.W. would minister to those who came in need of care to the Longcroft. John himself had been part of a Brethren assembly, and he had been taken to hear G.W. at the Longcroft by one of the elders of his church. It was a snowy winter's day at a sedate English house. He recounts how, sitting at the antique oak dining table, during a very formal meal, 'a white-haired gentleman' asked,

"Why are you here, young man?"

"Sir, I need the Lord to bless me."

"If you will open your heart, young man, I believe the Lord will bless you this evening."

'That night he preached on 1 Kings 8 - The dedication of the temple of Solomon. When the temple was made ready, though it was all finished, there was no God. The Ark of the Covenant had to be brought, and, when it was in place, the Glory of the Lord filled the temple. The Ark was Christ. With the consecration of our hearts, He would fill us with the Holy Ghost. There and then, my heart rose to God and I had an experience of the Baptism of the Holy Ghost, speaking in other tongues in the midst of my eldership in the Brethren, members of my family and friends from Warrington.'

Later, after leaving his job at the Longcroft, John and his family returned to Warrington and a Fellowship and Church Centre began to form there.

'Those were wonderful days for me,' says John.

It was at John's request that Sunday morning meetings began at the Longcroft, though the use of the house was not officially changed until several years later, after G.W. had left.

THE FIRST HOUSE CHURCH.

Meanwhile things were happening at a house in Queen's Road in Liverpool, rented by Norman Meeten. He had a great concern for the youth of the city and had opened the house up 'for young people to stay and have their needs met. The whole purpose of the house in Liverpool,' he says, 'was that it should be somewhere where all the kids I knew from around the city knew at least one place that they could come to and be welcome at any time.'

Norman knew many of these young people from his involvement

with World Friendship House during his ministry in the Liverpool community. He says that the Lord had shown him that the Church was not just a place for holding meetings; it was a place where people lived. Many of the young people who stayed at Queen's Road had been virtually homeless; some were drug addicts and alcoholics. Norman took some of them camping in Wales for two weeks, inviting G.W. to go and teach in the second week.

Years later, G.W. himself wrote a letter, describing what had happened At Queen's Road:

'With the purchase of independent premises in Liverpool, the work began to take new shape. The house was due for demolition and was acquired cheaply, with the knowledge that it could only be a temporary headquarters for whatever God wished to accomplish there. No-one had in mind that it would ever become a house church, or foresaw what would happen.

Soon a growing company of young people began to visit the place. Norman Meeten was still a curate of the Church of England and had no intention of starting a church. His oft-repeated statement at that time was, 'We are the handmaid of all the churches,' and the door was open to any who came along seeking help. Gradually he was joined by a band of lay assistants, willing to work with him for the reclamation of humanity.'

Until that time, Norman and G.W. had been holding regular midweek meetings at the Quaker Meeting House in Liverpool. They had used other church premises; but were not welcome because they were thought to be heretics; but the Quakers seemed not to mind what their beliefs were. Now a room was available at the house in Queen's Road and every Tuesday night it was packed with 'people seeking God'. G.W. was the main speaker at these gatherings.

'We recognised that he knew more than we did,' says Norman. 'The Lord had met us, but we realised that he had moved in these things for years before he ever came to us and therefore knew more than we knew. We were just hungry people, revelling in the fact that someone could teach us.'

G.W. continues his letter:

'At the same time a lady helper requested that a Sunday afternoon Bible class should be started for about a dozen girls in whom she was particularly interested. The first Sunday, this group of teenagers gathered in a room devoid of all furniture, and sat around the floor, backs to the wall, with Bibles open in front of them, for an hour's solid Bible study.

The next Sunday there was twice the number and the third Sunday many more; and so it went on. Soon the young men began to complain that they were missing out and so it became a mixed Bible class. Salvation, deliverance, healings became common occurrences; almost all who came were blessed and everyone who repented received a new heart, filled with the Spirit of God.

As news of the blessing spread people came from surrounding neighbourhoods to be filled with the Spirit and, before long, the room became too small. Doors were removed, the preaching stand was made in the doorway and people gathered on the landing. Soon the room opposite was filled and then the stairs leading to the upper floor and the ground floor. Every available space became jammed with people of all ages, eager for the word of truth and life.

It was all very thrilling. Every class of society was represented: social barriers were swept away. Hours would pass in the love and power and glory of the Lord. Some would say, "I wish it could go on for another hour," or, "No meeting should be less than three hours," as if to confound the pundits who say nobody can take more than twenty minutes of preaching.

It was the same on Tuesday evenings. To get into the meetings people had to come early and, when in, had to keep still, packed in without an inch to spare for at least two hours. God was moving; lives were changed; hearts made new; devils cast out; people filled with the Spirit. The insecure house creaked under the sheer weight of bodies. It was a wonder it did not collapse under the abuse. God held it together. It was all a miracle.'

All these meetings were held outside regular church hours. Norman Meeten still had his church duties to perform and was scrupulously careful that nothing should be done to infringe on his calling or in any way prevent people attending their own church services.

'Regrettably we did not escape criticism and a certain degree of persecution from some,' remembers G.W., 'but, despite it all, it grew until the house could no longer contain the numbers of people and it became necessary to find larger premises.

The work continued to expand in the new premises and, however many have been grieved by its success, the Lord certainly set His seal of approval on it. Hundreds were reached by the power of God. Some came to observe, some came to criticise; but most came to stay.' So, Queens Road became the first of the house churches.

G.W. told the story of the people who lived at Queen's Road under Rev. Meeten's care. 'Most of them had no church connections at all, so would lie in bed on Sunday mornings. So, rousing them up one such morning, he took them off to church. However, they refused to go again, creating a problem for Norman. Reluctantly, he agreed to open the house for Sunday morning services. Eventually, after Norman resigned his curacy, he became full-time leader of the Fellowship.

A church had come into being in the house. It was a spontaneous work of the Spirit of God. The charge was brought upon us by circumstances. We did not fully understand what was happening and were entirely without ambition. But, before long, the law of growth asserted itself and we were caught up in it as ready servants.'

As for Norman, he had spoken to his bishop about leaving the Anglican Church, mainly because he could not tolerate his duties with regard to infant baptism.

'I couldn't go on doing that,' he explains. 'At the last baptism I took all the godparents were drunk. When I took the certificate to the house where the baby was supposed to have been, they denied all existence of the child.'

Norman was chaplain to the maternity hospital where he had to go and sprinkle water on tiny, almost unrecognisable babies. He found this distasteful. Besides, he wanted to be baptised himself. But this was unacceptable, Norman says, if you had been baptised as an infant in the Anglican Church. People were told that when a baby was baptised, it became regenerate, made a child of God and an inheritor of the Kingdom.

When Norman had discussed his concerns with his bishop, the bishop had told him to wait six months before making a decision on his future. This he duly did before resigning his position within the Church. He remains able to take up his Anglican vocation again if he so wishes.

After that, G.W. was able to baptise him, with great pleasure!

DEVELOPMENT OF HOUSE CHURCHES

Norman Meeten tells how, whilst he was sitting at the table one mealtime at Queen's Road, the Lord gave him a vision. The vision was of a tree like a Canadian maple in autumn, covered with leaves that looked like flames. He recounts:

'All the leaves began to fall - not like a carpet, but in a heap. They glowed like the burning bush, not consumed. The wind began to blow and it pulled them up into the air. They became a canopy in the sky. Under this canopy was a globe; the leaves began to settle all over the globe.' Having asked the Lord what this vision meant, Norman received a reply:

'The tree represents the Tree of Life and the leaves represent the people. I'm going to allow you to come together and burn in love and then the wind of my Spirit will catch you up and scatter you to the uttermost parts of the earth, because the leaves of the tree are for the healing of the nations.'

At that time, Norman says that he did not know, until he read it three months later, that the latter part of this explanation was a verse from Revelation. 'There it was exactly!' he exclaimed. 'They were precisely the words that the Lord had spoken to me. Virtually from that time the Lord began to send people out.' Norman points out that the leaves did not refer exclusively to Queen's Road people.

In 1980 G.W. described how the house churches had developed in the 1960s through people coming to the Liverpool fellowship; eventually leaving to settle in other towns, there witnessing to what they had seen and heard and gradually gathering groups of others around them to form new churches. These were characterised by freedom of worship and ministry, which included the working of spiritual Gifts. There was no ordained ministry other than locally ordained elders. Each of these house churches was completely autonomous. There was no central government or administrative centre amongst this group; nothing of a hierarchical nature.

'Common need and mutual desire, as well as Scriptural command, draws and binds us together,' said G.W. 'We are linked by mutual consent only. There is no set pattern. The churches vary from place to place. Itinerant ministry from several of the more gifted brethren is available on application to them personally. A steady and growing stream of men and women go from house churches to other lands, the result being that house churches have sprung up spontaneously in other countries. This has not been our purpose, but it has nevertheless happened.'

G.W. gives as one of the main reasons why the house churches started was that they were of a loving, caring nature:

'People came because they were so disillusioned with both the standard of life and the quality of the ministry in the churches they were attending. The sight of people being delivered from evil spirits, bodies being healed and souls being saved in meetings was new and unknown to them. They felt they had been robbed; that scriptural love and power had either been withheld from or purposely denied them and they were not prepared to endure it any longer. Finer points of theology or doctrine ceased to mean so much to them as being involved in a church that moved in the power and demonstration of the Spirit, was knit together in love and sought to walk in holiness of life. This is what they found in the house churches and this is why they came.

God raised up the house churches to fulfil His will at this point in history. How long they continue to do so may determine their sphere of usefulness to the Lord and the length of their existence.'

In a letter to John Lewis of WEC. Missions in 1981 G.W. wrote that,

'Norman Meeten was the one around whom, in the beginning, the great work began. As for myself, I am merely a servant of the Lord and of the church. I am not working to any kind of plan or structure. I have no particular interest in setting up house churches. They just came about, so far as I am concerned. I am not in possession of God's blueprint, neither do I make any claims to knowing what His will is.'

Indeed, Norman recalls that, though G.W. had 'tremendous input' into house fellowships, he was not the initiator of any of them. In the John Lewis letter G.W. admits that he was 'fully engaged, mostly within the house church movement. But I do wonder whether indeed the house fellowship movement will be the prevailing one in the end times. I have

An Influential Preacher

no great yearning for it. It is only that my lot is cast in this way by the Spirit of God at this time. If He should move me out of them I would be most content. All I know is that I don't want to put labels on anything, neither do I want to get into another kind of rigid structure.'

It seems that GW. never wanted to be thought of as the initiator of a movement or a denomination; he always referred to Norman Meeten as 'the father of the Fellowships.'

One of the young men who went to the Queen's Road meetings was Fred Tomlinson, later a Fellowship leader in Canada and international Bible teacher. He was, at the time, a Liverpool policeman and describes how several members of his family, being Brethren believers, 'did the unthinkable and started attending meetings at the notorious House in the city. All were passionate about what they had found but I had considerable reservations. However, after some months, we decided to go and see what was happening. Little did we realise how that decision would impact our own lives and the lives of countless others in the years to come.

Among those who impressed us greatly was the main speaker, Mr. G.W. North. Upon hearing him, we quickly realised that he had an extraordinary authority in his ministry as well as remarkable insight into the truth of Scripture. As we became more acquainted with him, we discovered that his life was an uncommon expression of the love of God. It was so much more than words; it emanated from him.

It was an unspeakable privilege to experience the richness of the Lord's presence and to hear Him speak so clearly. I can say I never went home disappointed. There was certainly no famine of the word of God in those days!'

CONFERENCES

The Longcroft, as well as being a refuge for needy people, had started to become a conference centre. The conference programme began with monthly meetings. Then people would come and stay in the house and at Barnston Dale camp, down the road for the weekend to listen to G.W.'s and Norman's teachings.

At the first weekend conference in 1964 two women were miraculously healed whilst singing a hymn. No-one prayed for them. Many people who were to become leaders were blessed at those meetings.

'G.W. was the instrument of God's blessing to so many of us in those early days,' one of their number recalls. 'He brought the blessings of Bradford to us.'

In due course the conferences moved on to High Leigh in London, then to Swanwick in Derbyshire, to Cliff College in 1968 and eventually to Rora House in Devon. There they continue annually as the New Life Conference, convened for 'people who are hungry for the things of the Spirit'. For two weeks in August broadcasts on New Life Radio go out from the conference to many countries.

Of course the list of conference speakers has expanded to include other gifted preachers and teachers, and thriving youth and children's events have grown out of the main meetings. One of the conference days became given over entirely to missionaries, the whole ethos of the conference being to spread the word.

An elder writes from Canada:

'Cliff conferences were the highlight of the year for us. What glorious times we had! Wonderful, heart-warming preaching; and times when there was no preaching and we all hugged one another. {GW. used to say that more people got set free in those "Love-ins" than through all the sermons}'

Norman Meeten recalls one particularly powerful session at Cliff conference, when GW. had been preaching on The Fall of Jericho. He had said that more was accomplished with that one shout than all the deliverance that people were talking about. Then he said,

"Shout!"

'I have never heard people shout like that,' says Norman. Against people's advice, Norman had taken a young man to the conference with him. This young man was the son of a well-known architect and he was, Norman says, 'completely mentally ill.' He was unshaven and unkempt when he was taken to Cliff conference. People thought he should not have been there. Norman describes how, above all the shouting and noise of the meeting, 'there was this horrendous cry.' It was the young man as he clambered over everyone to get to the front. G.W. prayed for him, then told someone to 'go and put him to bed.'

'The next morning he got up as sober as you and me,' Norman reports. 'There was a very sophisticated lady sitting at the back of the meeting tent- very well-groomed. After the meeting she came to me and said, "For the first time in my life I feel normal." The conferences were tremendous times. They were remarkable, the things that happened.'

THE CHARISMATIC MOVEMENT

During his time at The Longcroft G.W. was able to preach and teach around the country. The Liverpool people set up venues for his ministry and he was introduced to a far wider circle than he had known in the Holiness churches. He chose not to become a church elder in Liverpool so that he could be free to travel and preach.

'People were so hungry in those days,' says Norman. 'The Spirit was moving in a remarkable way at that time; not only amongst us, but in the Anglican church.' This hunger for the things of the Spirit culminated in the setting up of the Fountain Trust. Similarly, there was movement in the Brethren church, where some leaders were 'read out' of their assemblies. These were some examples of the things that were happening at the beginning of the Charismatic Movement in this country. Things were also happening in the U.S. and New Zealand. 'We didn't realise the wonder of what the Lord was doing then,' says Norman. 'It is only in retrospect.'

At the time, Norman and G.W. were in contact with other men who were to become significant figures. In 1965 both men attended a conference at Herne Bay Court, the theme of which was 'The Apostolic Commission'. All the other men gathered there were to be instrumental and well-known in both the independent and denominational movements which ensued, but this was the last time Norman or G.W. went to similar get-togethers.

Soon the creation of house churches of many different 'flavours' became widespread. Their influence was felt in the traditional denominations, which saw them as divisive. But eventually the house churches came to be accepted as alternative and valid ways of conducting worship and church life, the established churches often using the concept of house groups within a larger set-up.

As the Charismatic Movement began to gather momentum, G.W.

found himself outside some of the structures which were being set up. For instance, he would not call himself an Apostle, as some of the leaders were entitled. He could not think of himself on the same level as the first Christian 'sent ones', though some have called him an apostle.

He became so concerned about the 'subtle authoritarianism' which he saw developing in some quarters that, in 1965, he felt obliged to do a very rare thing: write a circular letter on the matter to Fellowship elders associated with him. At the beginning of the letter he quotes from Peter - *The Elders which are among you I exhort - feed the flock of God - taking the oversight willingly - neither as being lords over God's heritage*, and Paul - *I give my judgement,[as one that hath obtained mercy of the Lord] to be faithful. - Not for that I have dominion over your faith, but am a helper of your joy.*

Here he apologises if he has fallen short in his duty to the elders: -

'If, at times some of you have felt I have to any degree neglected what I should have regarded as a duty to you all, or have withheld a ministry given by God for His people [and therefore expected of me by Him], I would say I wish to be faithful; I have no [and refuse to exercise] dominion over your faith; I believe that all rule among us is primarily by leadership and not by lordship; thus love reigns and not force. I would therefore that you adopt the same attitude to all the members of your flock.'

It may be said that G.W. was adopting the role of an apostle here, and aligning himself with apostles in this instance. However, in the letter he quotes George Fox, who once said that he was raised up of God to turn everyone to the voice of the Shepherd, who speaks in every heart. 'This is spiritual wisdom from a man of God,' says GW. 'Everyone must be free to listen to God direct.'

He goes on, 'Of course, there should be such an atmosphere of love and mutual trust and such should be the relationships in any fellowship that people will want to come and discuss with the elders their personal affairs. But if this is not so, 'tis folly to attempt to enforce it and no-one is bound to do so. Remember that if a man has to appeal to his office in order to gain respect or to establish his authority, he has surely forfeited it, and publishes the fact that he ought never to have been elected to that office in the first place.'

He exhorts those in office, 'To let care be taken that our manner and ministry does not warrant the accusation of intrusion into people's private affairs. You too, together with your flock, are being taught of God. Therefore refrain from legalistic dogmatism; allow the Lord to reshape your thinking. Renewal of the mind is the only way to transformation into His glorious likeness. Your duty is not to usurp the position of teacher, leader and Lord in any man's life, but to direct every man's awakened consciousness to Him, so that He may be to them all He wishes to be.'

Throughout his ministry, people would sometimes leave frustrated when coming to G.W. for advice on their personal affairs. He would hesitate to give them any specific guidance, 'Besides,' he would say, 'I might be wrong. Then if things went wrong in their lives, I would get the blame!'

Instead, he would encourage people to listen to the 'voice of the Shepherd' in their own hearts.

GUIDANCE

For himself, in 1967 G.W. had written:

'I have not, for these many years past, sought for extraordinary means of guidance. I have never thought I ought. I do not think it is right for me to ask special favours, tokens or interventions on my behalf. It is not my practice to seek special verses of Scripture, nor resort to the habit of 'fleece-laying', but rather to act on the assumption that, being born of God, I shall also be borne of Him.' He had admitted to having done this before going to Bradford. but had come to realise that he should not have done it.

'Why should I imagine I need any special guidance to change my lodging? It seems to me that to presume to be a Gideon or some other Bible character in this matter of guidance is surely to have this whole truth out of proportion as well as perspective. The mechanism of guidance is within each child of God. Recognition of this will bring confidence. I am a son of God, therefore sure to be guided of Him as I walk in that sonship; remembering that He is more desirous of His will being done in the world than I am; that is why He taught us to pray to that end.

Moreover, methods of guidance change with maturity. When Jesus was a baby His Father used dreams and voices to protect the child. When Jesus grew up He said, "I always do the things that please Him." Whilst we insist on means for babes we shall not find God uses the means for men. Paul said he *put away childish things.*'

This was what he believed. However, Wally and Dolly were to be in need of some personal guidance when they began to feel that their days on Merseyside were coming to an end. Wally felt that he wanted to be freed from his work at the Longcroft so that he could devote all his time to preaching and teaching.

With Norman Meeten

CHAPTER 6
A TRAVELLING PREACHER.

The direction that Wally and Dolly needed began to become clear when Wally met Bob and Norah Love. Wally had been invited to preach at a church at Farnham in Hampshire. The person who normally put him up was unable to do so and Bob and Norah Love agreed that they would be pleased to have him to stay. Norah had heard of GW. at a friend's house, where she had also heard for the first time about the Holy Spirit. She knew that she had found what she had been looking for, and the whole family had begun to seek for the Holy Spirit. Sometimes they would travel long distances in their search for the things of God.

On the morning GW. was due to leave after his preaching weekend, Bob went into his room to say goodbye before leaving for work. Whilst they were praying together GW. prophesied, saying that the Lord would take the pen out of Bob's hand and put a shepherd's crook into it. Later, Bob found out that GW had discovered a scrap of paper in his jacket pocket that he had forgotten about. On it he had scribbled that God had told him that he was to have more to do with this family.

At the time, Bob and Norah were attending an Anglican church and were fully involved in the work there. They had been baptised in the Spirit within a week of each other, Bob being delivered from his smoking and drinking problems. However, they expressed a wish to be baptised, following this experience, and were told that this was not acceptable for those already baptised as infants. Sadly, because of this, they felt that they had to leave their church. They caused quite a stir in the village when they were baptised in nearby Frensham pond. Eventually in 1965 they left Hampshire to work with an evangelist in Exeter.

Whilst they were trying to decide on whether to buy a large house, number 23 Belmont Road, Exeter, they attended a conference at Queen's Road fellowship in Liverpool. Norman and Jenny Meeten prayed with them about their decision and they returned to find that the price of the Belmont Road house had been dropped, with no explanation. Taking this as God's leading, they bought the house. They began to get involved with street evangelism, especially amongst the Mods and Rockers, finding that many young people came to join them in midweek prayer and teaching meetings. They were still attending a local church, but they were soon to be asked to hold their own Sunday meetings.

At their invitation, GW. would to go to speak at conferences in Exeter and, when Bob and Norah heard that he and Dolly were thinking of leaving The Longcroft, they invited them to make their home in Belmont Road, not expecting their invitation to be accepted. Reportedly, during an Exeter conference in 1967 Dolly remained in her room whilst a meeting was in progress, praying and seeking clarity on what she and her husband were to do. Maybe she did not share his confidence that all would become clear. At any rate, after the meeting Wally announced that they were going to move to Exeter, saying that the Lord had given him the direction he needed.

The development of the Fellowship in Exeter is just one early example of the beginnings of a house church connected with GW. Again, it was not intended to happen; it came about through circumstances and through people being blessed beyond the things they had previously known. Subsequently, two other houses adjoining the original in Belmont Road, were purchased and given over to this Fellowship.

One of the people who were blessed and helped at Belmont Road has written a booklet called 'A Labour of Love.' In it she recounts how 'Many people with deep needs, often of a spiritual nature, were delivered and set free from all kinds of bondages.' She describes the nature of the fellowship there as it began to grow:-

'There were no named elders and no structure of a church. No one made themselves appear to preside over another. Love was in action. The meetings were spontaneous. Nothing was pre-planned or organised; in fact, one didn't know what was to happen next, yet everything was orderly and under the Spirit's control. The Holy Spirit taught those who knew nothing, and there was an eagerness to learn and know God. There was a freshness and excitement. The uniting force was the love of Jesus; the evidence was the willingness to die to self and lay down our lives for each other.'

Amongst those joining the Exeter fellowship were several Christadelphian families. The father of one of these families had been quite a well-known lecturer in his circles. He and other leaders of their group, which met in Torquay, had many discussions about doctrine. They started to read books by authors such as Campbell Morgan and used Young's concordance to prepare sermons. Eventually, they began to question their central doctrines and to believe that these doctrines were erroneous.

This led a group of them to leave the Torquay assembly and begin holding their own Bible studies. It was a drastic thing to do and brought all sorts of accusations against them. Things changed when they came into contact with a man who had been in turn a Methodist and a Christadelphian. He was now running a house meeting in Paignton and invited the break-away group to join him. Consequently they decided to become part of his fellowship, gathering every week to 'break bread' with them. They took the step of being re-baptised; one of them, at least, in the Turkish Baths in Torquay!

A young preacher from the Exeter fellowship was invited to speak to the Paignton group. G.W., who had not yet moved from The Longcroft, was coming to preach at the Methodist church and one of the men from the group, after going to hear him, came back saying,

'We need to go to Belmont Road to hear Mr. North.'

'Quite a lot of things happened,' says one of their number. 'People spoke in Tongues; some received the Spirit and some didn't.'

One of the things that happened was that the ex-leader of the Christadelphian group bought number 25 Belmont Road, next door to the Fellowship house. 'He had a vision for a New Testament church,' says his son. The family moved into number 25 and proceeded to renovate the house for fellowship use. Amongst the renovations a flat was created for Wally and Dolly. The son of the family later married their daughter Marian, the young couple eventually becoming Fellowship leaders in Walsall before moving to missionary life in Zimbabwe.

Now the Fellowship owned three large houses and as the meetings grew it became necessary to knock down walls to accommodate people. They were beginning to sit on staircases, in a fashion reminiscent of Queen's Road days. One of their number recalls, 'The meetings were open for anyone to speak; the Gifts were in operation and people would get saved during meetings. There were nights of prayer; days of fasting were regular.'

Many people came to stay at the house; so there was lots of hospitality going on, perhaps most notably at the well attended Sunday lunches. People would often stay for afternoon tea as well. On a couple of occasions, two women described as 'witches' came to stay. One of these women, walking into the kitchen, fell to the floor. 'The powers she relied on to "read" people just wouldn't operate on those of us who were there and she lost her security and collapsed,' writes one observer.

During the building work a young man who had come for help climbed on to some scaffolding and fell, landing headfirst on the concrete below. 'An ambulance was called, but, by this time, the colour had gone from his face, his eyes were rolling and his breathing erratic. John [the builder] cradled him in his arms and cried out to God for him. By the time the ambulance arrived he was conscious, sitting up and the colour had returned to his face. He was kept in overnight for observation, then returned to the house, complaining of just a headache, the next day.'

Apparently, the Fellowship caused quite a stir at a nearby Bible College. Some of the students had been attending the Belmont Road meetings. On learning of this, the college ruled that the Fellowship was out of bounds, perhaps with good reason; some of their students were to become Fellowship leaders. Church leaders, missionaries and preachers of repute came out of those early days in Exeter. Bob Love described Belmont Road as a 'filling station' where he saw young people grounded in their faith and moving on.

NORAH LOVE REMINISCES

Norah Love remembers those years spent with Wally and Dolly with affection. She thought that, 'Dolly was the perfect wife for him.' She also says that, 'He was very wise and didn't go in for small talk, so some people thought he was unapproachable; but very few people knew him. He was good fun at things like parties and could appreciate good things and always showed appreciation.'

Sometimes Wally would be concerned about the welfare of those living and working in the Fellowship houses and would urge them to get into the car and drive out into the Devon countryside for the day. Sweets and ice cream were also prescribed. There could be too much serious stuff; some people needed normalising!

Norah says that she learned more from his [Wally's] life than his preaching.

To illustrate this she tells how GW. once borrowed a paintbrush from her and returned it cleaner than it was when he took it. 'That was typical of him,' she says. Once, when he was away, the old reclaimed cellar was decorated as a dining room. After having lunch in the new room, GW. commented, 'I wonder if this would have been too posh for Jesus!' Norah doesn't say whether the decorators were within earshot!

She goes on to tell how GW. had testified to her that before he was a Christian he had been a perfectionist. 'He could spot all the mistakes in something Dolly knitted him; but he missed all the love in the stitches. He said God had changed him. If he thought he had hurt someone, he was so sorry. He always showed gratitude for every little kindness shown him.'

She also talks of his 'generosity' to everybody, and, with regard to the accusation that GW. kept himself separate from other church elders she says that, 'People thought he tried to be different from the leaders of the other fellowships; but in Exeter the leaders got together in No. 23 Belmont Road. They wanted to see if they could sort out what they believed. Finally they had to agree to differ on doctrine, but they had a great respect for each other.'

THE LEAVES BEGIN TO FALL

During the late sixties and seventies house fellowships of varying natures were developing all around Britain. According to Joyce Thurman's 'New Wineskins,' there were three distinct strands of these fellowships, of which the Harvestime churches became the largest network, being more focused on expansion and structure than the others. She explains how the leaders of the various strands used to meet together at the earlier stages of development, but diverged as different strains of teaching and organisation emerged.

In his MA thesis Derrick Harrison lists 35 fellowships in Britain visited by GW. during the 1970s, as well as some in Canada, America, Cyprus and some African countries. He also mentions India, Nepal, Hungary, Germany and Australia. Other countries visited included Spain and Sweden.

These days the Exeter Fellowship meets in The Old Chapel, bought in the late '70s, after the meeting room at Belmont Road became too small. It had originally been a church; but was latterly used as a warehouse, now renovated as a church once more. Similar things happened to many house Fellowships, over the years. The fact that they no longer meet in houses is a tribute to their success. However, some original-style houses remain, offering hospitality and help, as well as meetings for worship, Bible teaching, preaching and outreach.

One couple, Pete and Joy Palmer, who bought No. 21 Belmont Road, had known GW. from his days in Kent. They had come to the Lord whilst 'propping up a bar' in the East End of London. Saturday afternoon meetings had started in their London home, at which Norman and GW. alternated, speaking at monthly meetings. This couple gave accommodation to Finnish people working in London, for which purpose they owned a very large house. But, again, the meeting rooms became too small. So, from there, they moved to a church hall in Crystal Palace and then on again to Penge.

Other London Fellowships at Eltham and Winchmore Hill arose from these meetings. By the time Wally and Dolly had moved to Exeter in 1968 Fellowships were developing all around the country. The leaves of the tree, spoken of by Norman, were beginning to fall throughout Britain.

At first, GW. spent his time itinerating, mostly within these groups. One three month period of his diary in 1971 includes Rora House conference[Devon], South Woodward[Chelmsford], London, Auchenheath[Scotland], Exeter[conference], Bulstrode[W.E.C. Headquarters, conference], Oldham, Warrington, King's Langley[Herts.], Winchmore Hill[London], Birmingham[two venues], Liverpool conference. Dolly would occasionally travel with her husband, but she usually preferred to stay at home and busy herself in the house. She would say that she did not like having nothing to do whilst her husband was busy; she did not relish sitting around all day, being waited on.

RORA HOUSE

During the early years of the Exeter fellowship Malcolm and Christine Ford were in process of buying Rora House, near Liverton in Devon. They had been farmers at Higher Whiddon Farm, Ashburton, regularly attending Ilsington Methodist Church. During the same period, they had started a fortnightly Bible Study in their farmhouse for those seeking Scriptural Holiness. The numbers meeting there grew rapidly and the people 'became hungry for the Holy Spirit, without realising what was happening.' Malcolm and Christine saw that the teaching they received about Holiness 'began to create a deep hunger in our hearts to be holy.'

After listening to a tape by David Du Plessis on 'The Baptism in the Holy Spirit' the couple finally knelt down one evening in the farm kitchen and asked God to baptise them in the Holy Spirit. Their lives began to be so transformed that all the young people they had led in the Christian Endeavour at the Methodist Church wanted to know what had happened to them. Some of these young people sought and found the gift of the Spirit for themselves. This was not well received by the church and, because of this, eventually a small group of them reluctantly resigned their church membership. A few months later, another group of young people turned up on the farm doorstep and the beginnings of a Fellowship began to form. Malcolm and Christine held their first conference in 1967, at which, they say, 'All were blessed of the Lord in a wonderful way, as they were all seeking a deeper walk with the Lord.'

At a gathering on a local farm in 1967, Malcolm and Christine met Bob and Norah Love. Bob and Norah invited them to a series of meetings led by GW. North at a Methodist Church in Exeter. 'We had never heard preaching like it, and were riveted to the seats, says Christine, 'We HAD to go on the second night. It meant more baby sitters, but we went.' From that day on they had a close connection with the Belmont Road Fellowship. GW. was invited to speak at the farm and he recommended other speakers. They remember that 'Every meeting was packed with young people, hungry for God. Many new people arrived each week.'

Though the spiritual work was flourishing, the farm was in financial difficulties; so much so that the Fords asked GW. to pray with them about their desperate situation. As they prayed together, they received a 'clear word from the Lord,' that they were 'a good tree, planted in bad ground.' Malcolm knew what he had to do: put the farm on the market.

Was there a connection between the tree Norman had seen at Queens Road and the one talked about at the farm? Now the people who had been given both these words from God had become connected and were to 'burn together' in Devon as well as in Liverpool, and send out many 'leaves' to different parts of the world.

Eventually Malcolm and Christine moved into Rora house at Liverton and began renovating it; fitting it out as a church and conference centre. Christine describes how, when GW. went with the couple to look at the house before it was purchased, he jumped up and down on the floorboards of the first floor before pronouncing it to be 'O.K.' She also tells how Dolly helped with scrubbing floors and how they 'received much counsel and words of wisdom from the Lord,' through her husband.

The house was opened up as a conference centre in 1970, GW. supporting and encouraging the Fords, urging them to press on, regardless of the many difficulties. Running the Fellowship and the conference centre was tremendously hard work; but Rora House became the venue for various and numerous conferences. These included youth camps and, most notably, from 1986, the large Summer Conferences. Cliff College had become too small and inconvenient to house the growing number of people attending.

PREACHING OVERSEAS

During his time in Exeter GW. began to extend his travels. His widening ministry led him to avail himself of secretarial services, offered to arrange and co-ordinate his appointments. His first invitation to preach abroad came in 1969 from Bethany Fellowship, a missionary society in Minnesota in the U.S.A. The following year he was invited to preach in India by Alan and Eileen Vincent. He and Dolly stayed with this couple in Bombay [now Mumbai] before travelling on to Darjeeling to fulfil speaking engagements in that area, arranged by a W.E.C. missionary, Hester Withey.

These were new and strange experiences for Wally and Dolly, now in their late fifties. They had never been abroad before and Dolly found the heat difficult to deal with. Another problem was that, as a matter of principal, Wally objected to immunisation. He had always felt that it was wrong to introduce even minute doses of an illness into your body and had never allowed his children to be vaccinated, a fact that they were to find problematical when they began to travel. Moreover, Dolly hated injections and was very ill after having her vaccinations before going to India. On top of that, she had always been frightened of dogs and was terrified when she heard of India's many wild dogs. But she was later to testify that God had delivered her from this fear whilst she was in India.

Having overcome these difficulties, the most trying thing in India for Dolly was having to drink gallons of Coke, which she hated! Coke was generally the drink offered to guests in India, so she could not have avoided accepting the despised beverage. Being away from home for months on end did not really suit her. She disliked travelling so much that Wally's future trips to India were made without her. He was to be accompanied by other men, who would be able to help with the ministry as well as keep an eye on the main preacher.

Dolly had never thought that she would ever travel abroad; but by 1984 had visited ten countries with her husband. Though she would sometimes be reluctant to go, Wally naturally wanted her to accompany him on at least some of his journeys, not least so that people could meet her. He thought people would think it strange if she was never with him.

'What am I going to do whilst you are busy?' was the question that bothered Dolly. In reality, she missed her husband badly when he was away. She couldn't wait for him to get home, though she was one hundred percent in favour of his going to 'preach the Gospel,' and was as dedicated as her husband to this cause. Hers was a life of sacrifice; but very cheerful sacrifice.

LETTERS FROM INDIA

Apart from some journals he kept in Australia towards the end of his life, some extracts from letters GW. wrote on an Indian journey in 1974 are the nearest things to a diary that he ever wrote. On this six month preaching tour Jack Kelly was travelling with G.W. and the letters were sent home to their wives. They are interesting in that they contain insights into some of G.W.'s own thoughts and feelings about the things that he was doing.

Bombay-25th November 1974 Yesterday at Byculla was a very blessed day. I ministered in the morning on The Foundations of the Temple, and in the evening on The Glory filling the Temple. Today is a 'rest' day for me. On Sunday I am to be at Bandra New Life Centre, which is the church that commenced in Alan's [Vincent] house in Chuim four years ago. On Wednesday I am to preach in St. Andrew's [Catholic] School to the Catholics. This is the first of a series of meetings lasting until Saturday. Then on Sunday I am due to go to Cabala Baptist for the day. After this, we fly to Kerala.

From Nepal. We travelled down to Rewa...We had a week of good outreach meetings. The Shamania was filled nightly with Hindus, Muslims and nominal Christians. The Lord reached many hearts and the response was real, so that eternal work was wrought in many hearts and we left rejoicing.

Bombay. On the first Sunday of arrival here I spoke three times; in the morning and afternoon to a Catholic Charismatic group that gathers fortnightly in this home. It was a most precious and amazing experience. They are the dearest, sweetest company you could meet. They just hung on the word and how they loved and worshipped the Lord! I was the only one who mentioned Mary and Peter; they were all 'Jesus.' Of course, they've just been born and they hunger and thirst after righteousness. Many of them have taken water baptism. Priests and nuns are among them. You'd love them. I rather think that Alan and Eileen are expecting something to happen as a result of these few days of meetings. They say there will be spies at the school taking notes of all I say, so I'm praying and looking for guidance and guardianship, so that I do not trespass beyond what the Lord wants me to speak, but I'm also expecting the grace to speak exactly what the Lord wants - Hallelujah! It's so obvious that these Catholics have been born again. Well, I'm looking forward to my assignment at the school. I'm told hundreds will come, and, if they advertised it, thousands.

At Nasrapur we had a small camp; most of the youngsters came from Calaba Baptist. Well, the Spirit just worked, that's about the best way to describe it. All sorts of things happened; healing, deliverance, New Birth, distribution of Gifts; it was a wonderful time. Charlie [the pastor] was so overjoyed at what had happened to his young people.

Sat. 30th The meetings at Byculla finish tonight and we're expecting a big crowd! They have grown nightly, and a deep hunger for the truth is gripping everybody. Last evening I spoke for two hours on The Bride, and the whole company just responded. It was very precious and moving. Tonight I am to speak to them on The Gifts. It is expected that the crowd will be larger than ever. We have had to rearrange the room. It's been wonderful to see the working of the Lord. We've both [he and Jack Kelly] been kept busy talking to people after the meetings.

Monday a.m. The meetings over the weekend have been 'wonderful,' to use Jack's expression.

Saturday evening was indeed a great time. The place was packed, with some standing. The response was whole-hearted. Perhaps 50 percent of the people were out at the front and much work was done in hearts.

When we arrived home Bernie [Hull] and John [Simkins] had arrived. It was great to see them again.

I preached at Bandra in the church which commenced in Chuim village when we [Dolly and Wally] were out four years ago together. Well, I preached four times [one for each year.] I was tired at the end, but it was all so abundantly worthwhile, for many sought the Lord. Again, the place was packed, some leaving for want of room, others standing inside and outside the building.

Yesterday Alan and Eileen held the final meetings among the Catholics here in their own house. After the last meeting the people went on to a party - a thirtieth wedding anniversary. They gave great testimonies to the New Birth; saying how they had been laying in some champagne and whisky for the occasion, but now all they wanted was Jesus and His people. It was a wonderful testimony to the Lord's grace and power.

Thurs. a.m. Last night I commenced my first meeting with the Catholics. We met in the gymnasium at St. Andrews school. There were 350 there. It was certainly a new experience for me. I've never addressed a totally Roman Catholic meeting before. It really was a sight to see 'Fathers' and nuns, beside the laity, joining in praising the Lord. Of course, these were not in the majority; the greater part were unsaved. I preached on The New Covenant and had liberty to declare the truth. Tonight I feel led to preach on Faith- taking the Kingdom by force. This opening is of the Lord and I want to take the opportunity granted me, for it may never come again. It looks as though things are heading up for a clash within the Roman Catholic set-up.

Alan and Eileen have laboured among them and there is undeniable fruit for their labours. But, sooner or later the Devil will kick, and then the fight will be on. However, there are those whose eyes have been opened, and, when opposition or persecution arises, will stand firm

Friday a.m. There was a bigger crowd last night, about 400. The response to the preaching was immediate and large. These people are wide open to the Gospel, needing no pressurising at all. Invitations to come to the Lord for healing are as quickly accepted as to seek Him for Salvation. Jack confesses himself to be amazed by it all. I spent yesterday afternoon visiting homes to pray for the sick and possessed. There is an awful amount of sickness among them or trouble of one sort or another. It's a real sight to see the saved ones dispersing among the unsaved at the end of a meeting and praying with them. I'm sure the Lord's heart is full of joy to see their fervour of love.

Saturday Well, the Roman Catholic meetings finished last evening. So many sought the Lord for all sorts of things. Following that, we all went off to a nun's house for supper, where again I was able to speak to a very attentive group who were eating sandwiches etc. Tonight I am due to go to Borivilli, where there is a mixed Catholic and Protestant company.

Monday a.m. This will be my last instalment. The meeting on Saturday was a real time of blessing. I'm glad I went. I preached on Faith. The impact was really tremendous and the response immediate.

Yesterday was my last preaching engagement in Bombay. It was a joy to be with them. My, what a change has taken place there! It's almost a mini-revival. The youngsters have gone on in the intervening days. The services have been revolutionised. There is a spirit of expectancy and excitement among them and the Lord is moving in the way we know. This visit has been the most blessed so far in the northern part of India.

I should think that over the whole time here some 750 [at a rough estimate; I do not count] have sought the Lord for one thing or another. In fact, the power of the Lord has worked on just about everybody that has been in the meetings.

..Well, it seems I must draw this epistle to a close.

..We do praise God constantly for the privilege of being allowed to minister here in these days of blessing. We are allowed to join in the reaping, perhaps, where others have sowed, but the joy of harvest is nonetheless sweet.

26-12-74—Delhi. Our stay in Bombay concluded with meetings at Borivilli. The meetings were the first of a series they hope to continue between 'Charismatics' of all denominations. The day we spent among them was precious. The order of service-hymn, prayer, hymn etc. - has died, and spontaneity and life are in evidence. It was a pleasure to be among them.

Jack [a heart surgeon] is spending each morning at the local hospital. He is being used to the full and seems to be enjoying it. It is Brethren foundation and the chief is a fine surgeon who esteems Jack very highly. Everyone thinks he is wonderful and is clamouring to be seen by him.

A Travelling Preacher

You may be sure, then, how great a blessing he is to these people.

I felt that the Lord wished me to take a series on The Unity of the Spirit for the morning sessions and in the evening, a series of themes connected with The Will of God. So, for the past fourteen days, I have been giving two-hour talks morning and evening on these topics, and still I haven't finished. I spent four mornings, eight hours in all, on the 'One Baptism.' At present I am doing, 'One God and Father of us all.' I've been greatly blessed to be able to spend so much time on the theme so dear to my heart and can see the usefulness of such an exercise. Cherian has requested to have the book [One Baptism] when it is finished, asking my permission to have it published in Malayalam. Besides this, I have been out to other meetings, travelling long distances, and the Lord has worked in many [hundreds, it seems] lives.

Fri. 27th Dec. Well, it's Friday. I've finished the 'school.' This morning I wound up the series on 'The Unity of the Spirit.' The Lord has richly blessed me in speaking on this series. These people have obviously received the truth, which has systematically grounded and built them up in the Faith.

Sat. 28th Dec. It is now over three months since arriving in Delhi and what a time it has been. The time will soon slip away for us, for we shall be kept hard at it everywhere, and may the end be glorious for the Lord. This morning I received a card stating that since the conference in Khatmandu ten families in one place, comprising fifty people, have requested to be taught the Word.

I'm told I am to speak at two meetings tomorrow; one the annual fellowship meeting of a local evangelical group [St. Thomas Evangelical Churches], and the other the opening meeting of the C.S.I. [Church of Southern India] convention. The Bishop is to be there. The old Bishop Athanasius, who invited us to his 'palace' to tea, when we were last here, has passed away.

Mon. 30th Dec. Yesterday was a day of bishops at both places.

Tues 31st Dec. There's no doubt about it, these people get as much into every day as they can, rising before 5a.m. The first meeting commences at that hour <u>every day of the year</u>. They sing and then pray. That's the way each day begins. And, when you think that I shall not begin preaching tonight until about 8.15, and will go on for an hour or so, before returning here at around 10-10.30 p.m., you can get some idea of the length of the day. Of course, it isn't always convention time, but they're always up in the morning. It's never cold here. They're never tempted to stay in bed in the warm, as we are; but these Malalis really are industrious people. They pack their days with activity of all sorts.

2nd Jan. Yesterday was a quiet, restful day, except for a surprise meeting – a New Year message to the Y.W.C.A. at Triuvalla. One is never quite sure what the day may bring forth.

4th Jan. Last night I preached at a big convention at which Cherian said there were 1900 women alone, to say nothing of the men. Countless hundreds stood at the invitation, which was made without pressure. Just what happens is hard to tell, for contact is impossible, there being no conversational exchange. Only the Lord knows what are the effects of it all. So long as we do not labour in vain, all will be to His glory.

REFLECTIONS ON HEALING

As indicated in the diary letters, GW., in common with any preacher visiting India, was asked to spend some of his time praying for the sick. He remembered that on one of his visits, Jack, he had landed with Jack in the South of India, looking forward to his scheduled two day rest period.

'When we landed,' he related, 'a man said, "You wouldn't mind speaking to a veranda meeting tonight, would you?" The verandas run all round the house - very wide. People were sitting close together. There were hundreds of them! Doors were open to the house. People were stacked up inside and there were rows of them outside as well, Jack says at least a thousand. It's nothing to speak to thousands in the South of India. Don't think that's a marvellous thing. You could go and have a couple of thousand to hear you, just the same. You do very well if you get ten in the North.

They had built a kind of platform, and I spoke for twenty minutes. Many people responded to the preaching of the Gospel and that was that. Then this man stood up and said,

"Now Brother North will pray for you for healing." Hundreds of people stood up. Three a minute were coming for two hours. That's the only sort of healing meeting I have ever been involved in, and that was arranged by someone else, and God worked."

GW. told this story at Auchenheath to emphasise the fact that he did not have the Gift of Healing. 'Some people have that Gift and they have a responsibility before God to use it and render their account for it,' he said.

THE HEALING OF THE LEPER

Many years later GW. was asked if he would relate some of the interesting stories of outstanding events in his life. He rarely used these as illustrations during preaching, aware that doing this might sound like boasting. At this particular meeting in Warrington G.W. was asked to tell the story of the healing of the leper in India, and agreed to do it, as, he said, 'Others have told it, but I find it has not always been told correctly.' He admitted then that his own power of recall wasn't quite what it used to be.

In his own words:-

'I went to a place called Pokhara, up in Nepal, to a little place called the Shining Hospital. It is built of aluminium, which reflects the sun, hence its name. Further down from this hospital is another one called Green Pastures. This is a leprosarium. In those days, as soon as a person had leprosy, he knew nothing but his leprosy. By common consent, his wife turned him out; no-one would go near him; his own children wouldn't look at him. He became an outcast; a penniless beggar, having nothing in this world, cast out as dead. So when you preached to a leper, you were preaching to someone who was ready for the Gospel.

The particular man of the story arrived at Green Pastures on Sunday during the morning service, which was to be my last meeting there. My interpreter and I were to leave immediately after lunch to get down to the airport.

What a day that was, and what a meeting! [I think it was at that meeting that Debhu Singh, my interpreter, dropped to his knees and begged God to meet his need]. As the meeting closed, I gave the company an invitation to respond, and Oh, how they did! I shall never forget it. One poor, disfigured man raised himself up, dragged himself to the front weeping, and immediately became an evangelist. Turning round to his fellows, he said,

"Come on, come on!" I couldn't understand him; but they did. They came. He'd only been saved about a minute or so. Eventually, the matron of the hospital came up to me and said,

"Will you come and pray with a man who has just come in? He's going to die unless God heals him. He's too far gone. We can do nothing for him. He has come from a village right up in the mountains. He's only just managed to drag himself here. He has found us at last; but it's too late. We can't do anything for him."

I went to the hospital. It was a long whitewashed room, divided into cubicles. The missionaries had done as much as they could with the meagre resources they had been sent, while people were buying and furnishing big houses in England. The man was in a cubicle just near the entrance. It was very small; there was no bed; you wouldn't have kept your dog in it. You love your dogs, don't you?

The poor man sat back on his haunches; isolated; immune from everything except himself and his disease. I was looking at a man dead on his feet. He was a terrible sight, but he sat there without a whimper. Not knowing what else to do, I said to the matron,

"Tell him I'm a servant of the Lord Jesus Christ." She told him.

"Now I want you to tell him that, if he will believe, Jesus Christ will heal him."

"You do understand, don't you, that he's never heard of the Lord Jesus Christ. How can you expect him to believe in a person of whom he's never heard?"

"It doesn't matter whether he's heard about Jesus before; he's hearing about Him now. Just tell him, sister." So that lovely soul [How she cared for those lepers!] told him. There was no sign of recognition on the poor man's face. He sat there imperturbable – lost somewhere behind the pain barrier, I suppose. I said,

"Will you now tell him this – he must believe in Jesus Christ alone if he wants to be healed."

"But he's been taught to believe in hundreds of gods. From a child he has worshipped his gods. You can't expect him to believe now. He's never heard the name."

"Never mind; you tell him that. He knows his gods have done nothing for him. He's lost every thing; he's got nothing; he knows that. You must tell him that he must believe on Jesus Christ and on Jesus Christ alone. I can't pray for him if he's believing on all the rest, plus Jesus Christ." She told him what I had said. For the first time he made a response, nodding his head. He understood. I turned my thoughts to the Lord.

"Lord," I said. "Lord, I'm leaving here. I want them to be able to pray for lepers after I'm gone. It's not just me praying. We'll use the James five method. Will someone go and get some oil." Away went the matron and came back with some oil. I anointed him and said,

"Now, put your hands on him with me, sister." We put our hands on him together and prayed one short and softly spoken prayer; that's all. The Lord cleansed him. I never saw the completion of the miracle. I only saw the beginnings of it. Thankful for what I had witnessed, I left and dashed off to lunch and the airport.

I never went back to the leprosarium for a year; but my thoughts often went back to that wonderful occasion. As I travelled on, unknown to me, there was a letter following me around India, but never reaching me till I got back to England. It told me that the man was utterly cleansed.

In due course, I went back to Pokhara. I wanted to see this man. I had never seen a leper healed before. I had read about it in the Bible; but had never witnessed the miracle. Arriving there, looking for him, I was told he had gone. I thought all my hopes were dashed.

"It's not like that," the matron said. "He was cleansed and healed. He didn't know the Gospel, but he went round the camp telling everybody what Jesus had done for him. He just said what he knew. We taught him to read, and he became a great witness for the Lord Jesus among his own people. Just a few weeks ago he collected as many New Testaments as he could, and he's gone back to his village to preach Jesus to them.'"

After telling this story, GW. finished his talk in Warrington by proclaiming,

'If you will, you can come into clear knowledge of God and His ways. Not to do so is death worse than leprosy!'

ONE BAPTISM

Whilst he was in Kerala, India, in 1972, the subject of a book he had been writing had obviously been so much on G.W.'s mind that he recorded some of his thoughts on it. He had begun writing the book 'One Baptism,' published in 1978, whilst at home in Exeter. The title is taken from Paul's statement in Ephesians - *There is One Lord, one faith, one baptism* .This book is regarded as containing the central and definitive theme of G. W.'s teaching, setting out what he saw life under the New Covenant to mean. He would preach the chapters to the Exeter folk and gauge their reactions. For the writer the subject of the book had been the cause of much soul-searching as well as Scriptural research:-

'In connection with the book I am in process of writing on the One Baptism, God keeps exercising me along these lines. Certain it is that, as a result, I am more than ever convinced of the correctness of the conclusions to which I have already come [which in itself is clear enough that if a thing be true it has nothing to fear from intensive investigation].

Considering Luke 24 29, I saw that there could be two events referred to:

1. A reception of the promise of the Father, and:

2. An enduement with power from on high.

This is the current popular doctrine being propounded during the so-called 'Charismatic Revival.'

If it be true that there are two different experiences to be entered into at two different times and upon two separate occasions, then all I believe to be true about the One Baptism is incorrect, for this would show that there is a God-given and Scripturally based proof that I am wrong. I told the Lord that I was quite willing to withdraw and publicly renounce what I had been believing and preaching these years, if what this verse appeared to allow was really true.

Most people who preach the Baptism in the Spirit believe that it is an experience to be gained subsequent to Regeneration. That belief I have these many years believed to be false and not Scripturally founded. The general teaching is that by receiving the gift of the person of the Holy Spirit a man is Born Again, and that by being baptised in the Spirit a man is either entirely sanctified or empowered for service, or both.

Conversely, I believe and preach that the gift of the Holy Spirit and the Baptism in the Holy Spirit are but two aspects of one and the same thing, the former being the greater of the two. The latter is but a method used by God to impart the gift of the Holy Spirit at the same instant as the whole nature and personality is baptised in Him.

The Baptism is but a momentary thing [comparatively], but the impartation and indwelling of the Holy Ghost in fullness is for eternity. The baptism is the moment of regeneration, leading to the substantiation of the Person and life of the Son of God. Of this I am utterly convinced, even though among teaching brethren I may stand almost alone.'

So, he remained convinced of the truth that had dawned on him in Bradford in the midst of a time of revival. In his own words –

'The deeper the thought, the clearer the understanding. Any revelation from God is understanding by insight; but the Lord does not only give by revelation, he gives education also. The revelation is capable of explanation and therefore communicable.'

NOT FOR SALE

Although travelling around preaching and teaching was undoubtedly his forte as well as his great love, G.W. spent many, many hours putting down his thoughts in writing. In doing this he was responding to some of his listeners, who urged him to publish his teachings for the benefit of future generations. So, whilst continuing to fulfil many preaching engagements at home and abroad, between 1971 and 1992 GW. wrote 22 books of varying length, some of them no more than extended pamphlets. He also penned a couple of tracts for distribution. He would never allow his books to be published for sale. Whilst this may have limited their circulation, he believed that the preaching of the Gospel in any form should be without charge. The books were privately printed by Fellowships in Bradford and Exeter, and were labours of love for the editors and printers as well as the writer.

It was indeed laborious for those who had to decipher GW.'s notoriously indecipherable handwriting. G.W. himself spent the hours writing; not at a desk or table; but sitting in an armchair in the living room, often with Radio Three playing classical music beside him. His ever patient wife sometimes grew tired of the hours and hours of music, for which she did not share her husband's taste. She did not totally approve, either, of his rising at around 4 a.m. most mornings to continue writing and preaching preparation. She thought he could have gone back to sleep if he had tried; but he insisted otherwise, and no doubt the extra hours of work paid off. Besides, in later life, a snooze in the afternoons made up for the lack of sleep.

Books were not the only form of writing G.W. was engaged in. Personal problems were not ignored. Letters would sometimes arrive from people with needs of all kinds and he would spend hours and hours corresponding with those who sought his help and counsel, toiling over his replies. He was never too busy to listen to those who found life difficult. They talk of his compassion for them, seeking to bless them in both written and spoken words.

Many claim to have been greatly blessed and some even converted through reading GW's books. But others have found them very difficult to read because of their somewhat involved language. One person who has studied his sentence construction has observed,

'On average these days there are thirteen words in a sentence. On average GW's have sixty four words. He was from the generation of the King James Bible, which has these long sentences. If you've been trained with them you can hold these things in your mind because you know where the sentence is going; but modern generations can't. People can't cope with more than fifteen words at a time.'

Perhaps the most popular of his books has been 'The Representative Man' [1976] maybe because it is so short and compact. In it Jesus is portrayed as representing us in His life and death.

One book which has proved somewhat controversial is on the subject of Eldership [1979]. G.W. preached on this topic in Exeter, whilst no doubt dwelling on the theme for a book, and promptly made the fledgling elders there want to resign, so high a standard did he uphold for the office! However, they must have calmed down for they all carried on with their duties.

In one of G.W.'s publications 'A Sign of Authority' [1976, revised 1989] the writer sets out his reasons for insisting on the wearing of head-coverings by women in his meetings. Of course, during the time of his pastorates it was customary for women of all denominations to wear hats to church. But, as time went on, this practice was gradually discontinued in most churches, as being simply a cultural necessity in Bible days, though not in modern times.

Not so to this preacher. His question was,

'Do all realise that in challenging God's order, [1 Corinthians, 11]whether in Paul's day or modern times, churches are rebelling against God's institution? Whenever this is done, God Himself is being called into question, and to do this is very serious indeed.' To him it was a matter of obedience and portraying submission to God's order in the family and in the church and therefore something to be done wholeheartedly.

The matter did, of course, come in for some questioning and argument; but head-covering is still accepted in and characteristic of most of the Fellowships connected with GW.'s ministry, though not fanatically insisted upon. Indeed GW. himself, at a question and answer session, cautioned against taking the practice to ridiculous lengths. He had heard that in one church they kept a stock of headscarves at the back and gave them to any woman who came in 'uncovered', especially during times when people were seeking prayer for deliverance from evil spirits.

This may have happened because GW. had been known to declare in a meeting where he was praying for people for deliverance that he would not be responsible for any woman whose head was uncovered when demons were active. People naturally wondered what this meant and he was astonished when some thought that he was saying that demons could get in through the head. Of course, he was talking about the state of a rebellious heart, which might put people in danger.

There were other instances where his words were misunderstood and misapplied, sometimes rather comically. For instance, he once declared at a conference that he didn't like the wearing of wooden clogs, which were fashionable for women at the time. One girl who was present immediately stopped wearing her clogs, perhaps thinking that GW. had some spiritual reason for disliking them. She was surprised to find out that it was just the clattering noise they made which slightly irritated the preacher!

Another time GW. spoke against the wearing of black clothes, associating them with witches. As a result there is a certain gentleman who, even to this day, will not wear black shoes! These examples seem to back up the view expressed by Joyce Thurman in her Study of the House Church

Movement in 1982 that 'As Mr. North travels around the fellowships he is shown respect almost amounting to reverence by members.' Be that as it may, instances such as these were the subjects of incredulity and amusement to his family, who could scarcely believe the extent to which some individuals hung on their father's words.

It has also been noted that some of the young preachers associated with GW. would copy his mannerisms and style of preaching, without noticing that they were doing so. This was sometimes amusing and sometimes regrettable, but perhaps inevitable to a degree, though not wished for by the original.

It is true that GW. was treated with a great deal of respect by most of the people that he met during the course of his preaching life. Perhaps, to some degree, this was as a result of his being of an older generation than most of them and treated them in a fatherly fashion. Furthermore, many regarded him as their spiritual father.

SOME OF THE FALLING LEAVES

EPSOM

One church which sprang directly from the Exeter Fellowship grew up because Tony Seaton, a young lecturer at Exeter University, took up a teaching post at Epsom College, a boys' public school. He and his wife Mary had met at Exeter Fellowship and married in 1971 at their Parish Church. Mary remembers that, before she left Exeter, GW. prayed for her, that she would become 'a mother of boys away from their mothers.' And so it proved to be. She and her husband began to run the Christian Union on the college campus, working in conjunction with the college chaplain. There they held house parties in which they were joined by groups of students invited from other local schools.

When GW. was invited to speak at one of these, he found, to his surprise and delight, that he already knew the chaplain's wife, Mavis. She was the daughter of an old friend with whom he had worked when he had been in the wood business in Plaxtol. She had, of course, been a child the last time they had met.

Soon Tony and Mary needed premises in which to house a growing church. To their amazement, in an area known for expensive properties, they were offered a large house for very little money. This house belonged to a couple from Epsom Methodist Church, who felt led by the Lord to offer their house to Tony and Mary at a very cheap price. These generous people explained that they weren't interested in the money, but wanted their house to be used for Christian work. Their wish was fulfilled when eventually the lounge of their house became the Fellowship prayer room. The work became not only a thriving church, supporting many overseas missionaries, but a school, staffed by members of the Fellowship, which has been a haven for many families for more than twenty years.

BIRMINGHAM

One of the Fellowships in Birmingham began with 'an eager group of newly converted teenagers,' who were meeting at a little mission hall in the Sparkbrook area of the city. Their new-found joy found expression in evangelising around the pubs on Saturday evenings; Sunday afternoons being devoted to fellowship and Bible study. They would also travel to Liverpool to join in the meetings there and listen to G.W. North, returning 'excited and eager to translate what they had seen and experienced into their own gathering.'

Meanwhile, in the autumn of 1969, another small group was meeting at Birmingham Bible Institute, seeking the Lord for the Baptism in the Holy Spirit. Two of the students, who came from Warrington Fellowship, took several others from the B.B.I. group to Liverpool 'to see what was happening there and to hear this man who had been spoken of in reverential terms.' Derrick and Barbara Harrison, missionary trainees, were amongst this group of students. Derrick describes how, although 'Mr. North was not at the Liverpool meeting, Norman Meeten testified how he had come to God for deliverance from sin. This was music to my ears [having a Holiness background] and there and then I committed myself to this work of God.'

The two small Birmingham groups began to meet together, joined by several Christian University students, who had been touched by the Holy Spirit in a mission conducted by Roger Forster. These things happened at the beginning of the Charismatic Movement, when many college Christian Unions were experiencing renewal. Derrick reports:

'Quite a number of these University students became key members of our fellowship, several of them becoming leaders. We had no idea that eventually the small group of young people who met in our home would become a church. We simply met together because we felt strongly that it was God's will to do so and because we were so hungry and expectant that God was about to do something. As God poured out His Holy Spirit upon us, we discovered the joy of singing Wesley hymns, [picked up from our association with Liverpool]. We met informally, believing that we were inspired and led directly by the Holy Spirit. He led one and another to share Scripture and to speak in prophecy, tongues and interpretation. These were wonderful days, when we enjoyed richness of fellowship together in the Body of Christ. Whenever we saw needs among us, one or other would quickly supply what was needed. We truly loved one another in the Lord Jesus.

We were all young people and so had no older men to lead and guide us. For the first couple of years we met in homes and hired public meeting rooms. We met all day on Sundays and three times in the week for evening meetings. All the meetings were spontaneous – we lived for these times when God would be so real to us. We experienced growth through the witness of our own members and by the addition of those, newly awakened by the Holy Spirit, who recognised that God was with us in a special way. Such was this awareness of the Lord among us that several people moved from different parts of the U.K. to join us.'

When Barbara and Derrick finished Bible School in 1969, they went to the U.S.A. to complete missionary training. Derrick continues: 'The Fellowship grew, and Mr. North was invited to visit. When we returned, everyone was talking about him and his teaching concerning the New Birth and the Christian life. We found it more and more difficult to reconcile our responsibilities in the emerging house church with our commitment to our missionary society; but the crunch came when we had to resign over our commitment to Spiritual Gifts, especially Tongues.

When the church had grown to sixty adults and thirty children, Derrick left his job to get involved with the pastoral demands of these new believers. We had bought our own home as a place for the church to meet, but soon the neighbours began to complain about the noise and the number of cars. We were threatened with court action and so continued to meet in rented halls.'

Needing a much larger place to meet and having the Liverpool Fellowship house church as their model, the members decided on a plan of action. They called it a 'squeeze', which meant that they lived on the basic minimum of food and clothes for six months, so that they could give a specific amount of money each month towards a fellowship house.

Of course, all the children were adequately fed and clothed, but all the adults were included in the 'squeeze.' One family, after they had decided on the amount to give each month, only had enough left to buy one loaf of bread and one pint of milk per day.

Derrick and Barbara added to the funds by selling their own house. Eventually the church found a large house in the Harborne area and discovered to their joy, on viewing the property, that it already had planning permission for religious meetings. Now there was no possibility of the council closing them down! They felt this was a sign of the Lord's provision.

This fellowship has used this method of special sacrifice through 'squeezes' several times in order to meet specific needs with regard to church, mission and social necessities. On one occasion someone visited the fellowship from Eastern Europe and went home with carloads of clothes. Everyone had given practically every thing except what they were wearing; one person even put his wedding ring into the offering! This began a ministry into Eastern Europe which sparked off a number of other ministries.

Twelve years after moving into the house in Harborne this fellowship made the decision to move from the more prosperous area of Birmingham, where they had been situated, to Smethwick, a much poorer area, where they felt that they could reach more people. Another 'squeeze' was put into action to raise money for a new church building and minister's house. All the families sold their homes and moved to within a twelve mile radius of the church, several families putting their children into local schools. Derrick recalls how 'Mr. North proudly opened the new church in January 1987. The members of the fellowship had sacrificed not only their financial resources, but together we had worked for one whole year; every evening and every Saturday, to build the church and the pastor's house at the rear. The only outside skills we employed were the bricklayers and the plasterers. Other fellowships also came to help us build.'

Derrick tells us that 'Probably the greatest input of G.W. North into the fellowship came about through the Christian Workers' Programme [CWP.] The vision for teaching and training future leaders was the focus of a particular Elders' Conference, chaired by Mr. North, who felt that it was important to establish such a programme. When I visited him at his home in Bracknell and shared my vision and plans he encouraged us to proceed and he introduced the programme to other fellowships with a video presentation. From January 1993 he systematically taught and expounded New Testament books. He was, by now, elderly, but he loved to sit for two hours each day and share the rich wealth of his teaching and the fruit of his years of preaching and waiting on God. Students from various fellowships and from many different countries of the world benefited from this unique experience. He sat at a table with his Bible and the students around him. He was at his very best; but was completing his last years of ministry.'

LONDON

One of the larger Fellowships with which GW. was associated began with a meeting on a train. Terry Watson was travelling to work in central London when he met a member of the Exeter fellowship, who invited him to a gathering at the home of Pete and Joy Palmer at Crystal Palace .According to a letter from Frances, Terry's wife:-

'We arrived that evening to find that some of the walls of the room in the flat had been removed and curtains put in their place so that there could be maximum space for people to crowd into the meeting. Although we understood little of most of the beginning, when Mr. North stood up to preach we found ourselves riveted. This was something we had never heard or experienced before in the Baptist Church. We just knew it was something we desperately wanted.

Quarterly meetings were held in South Norwood. Here we entered into the reality of the fullness of the Lord; something our hearts were searching for, but we hadn't realised until now exactly what that was. These gatherings began to be known as 'The London meetings.'

In February 1971 we began meetings in our own home. Mr. North would visit each quarter for the London meetings, but at the same time the church in our house was developing fast with people visiting us for help and ministry. Some were involved in spiritual problems beyond our experience. Mr. North was often on hand to help us. His experience and knowledge of God, together with his discernment, were extraordinary. Many of the meetings we had with him were charged with power. Many needs became apparent whilst he was with us and we learned so much regarding deliverance in people's lives.

In 1974 Terry made his first overseas trip with Mr. North and Martin

Williams to Cyprus. During the first week they were all working together and the second week there were just Terry and Martin. The sense of the presence of God in the meetings had been outstanding. Terry assumed that without Mr. North this would continue, but later he noted that 'the presence of the Lord went with him,' a reminder as to how much the Lord was using Mr. North at that time.'

Frances ends her letter by saying,

'His impact on our lives and the lives of our family can never be measured. Our boys always enjoyed his visits and often talked personally with him. The Apostle Paul said to the church at Corinth that there were many teachers but not many fathers. We will always consider him to be a father in the Faith.'

CYPRUS

The Fellowships which sprang up in Cyprus became destinations Wally and Dolly particularly loved to visit. As well as the wamth of the sun, they revelled in the wonderful warmth of the hospitality they found, especially in the home of 'Mamma and Papa' Photiades. An account of the way in which the work began there is given by one of their sons, John Photiades, who became one of the church leaders:-

'I first met Mr. North when I was a student at the University of Newcastle Upon Tyne in January 1970. He was a guest speaker at the Christian Union where I was a regular attendant. When I saw and heard this white-haired man speaking I thought,

"This is it!"

It was what I had been searching and thirsting for during the preceding two years. I enquired whether this man was Norman Meeten, who I heard was coming to minister at the C.U., only to be told that this was Mr. North; Norman was coming later.

On the following day Mr. North read from Exodus 20: how God ordered that the altar should not be made with steps going up. He said,

"God made it easy for you; you can just fall on the altar." At the end he invited any to whom God had spoken to respond to the word. I did; and what followed was regeneration. What started then is going strong nearly 39 years later.

Six months later I finished my studies and returned to Cyprus, my home country. My parents and two brothers came to the Lord and eventually we started regular meetings in my father's house. Mr. North came to us to minister the word of God in 1974. This was the first of many visits over the years, during which we were eventually established as a church.

Coming from a nominal Christian background, we had no idea what and how a New Testament church should be. Mr. North was there at all the crucial times to guide us and stand with us. I often thank the Lord for our brother's faithful and loving ministry. He spoke the word of God; and this word is incorruptible seed. His last visit to Cyprus was in 1993.

In recent years I spent some time recording messages for transfer to CD.s and MP3 players and in the process, listened to many of the messages again. I discovered, to my amazement, that it was all so fresh; delightfully familiar; not in head knowledge, but in living realities. His word that His servant spoke is not lost; it has come to fruition.'

AN APOSTLE?

Fred Tomlinson, of Liverpool and Vancouver, has written of GW. that, 'Although he strongly resisted the title, both Mr. North's calling and stature were unmistakably apostolic. One of his arguments against accepting that designation was that he has never founded a church, but numerous men in leadership positions in many countries can trace their spiritual roots to the ministry of Mr. North.

The authority that this man commanded was not only recognised by his listeners, but also by demonic spirits. A clash between the kingdoms of light and darkness was not uncommon in his meetings Often he would not use the common phrase, "In Jesus' name." Instead, just the words, "Get out!" were enough to cause deeply entrenched spirits to be exposed and expelled.'

Another Fellowship elder testifies that his wife was delivered from the fear of depression through GW.'s discernment. He describes how the couple were just sitting chatting to GW. in their house, when he suddenly, out of the blue, asked, 'My dear, did your mother suffer from severe depression?'

'Yes, she did.'

'Let me pray for you.'

This lady had lived in fear. Both her mother and brother had had severe breakdowns and, whenever there was pressure, the greatest pressure for her was the fear that she too would break down. Her husband says that she became a 'different woman' as a result of that prayer. 'I've got my wife because of your father,' he told G.W.'s eldest daughter.

The same elder describes a visit to someone neither he nor GW. had met before, but whom GW. had heard was having 'some kind of demonic problems.' The two men went and sat down in the lady's house and the first thing GW. said to her was,

'Did your father see leprechauns?' She went as white as a sheet and replied,

'He always said he did, but none of us took him seriously.'

'Your father has seen the physical manifestation of demons. They are troubling your family. Let me pray for you.'

Back in the car, GW. explained, 'Sometimes the discernment just kicks in.'

'That is one of the reasons why I think he was an apostle. I think it's possible for all the gifts to be made manifest in an apostle. Whatever's lacking in a church, the apostle can make up for it,' is the opinion of this Fellowship elder.

Whilst G.W. undoubtedly manifested many apostolic gifts, he was careful not to let people think of him more highly than he felt was justified. One of his daughters was taken aback on one occasion, when she had been with him as he was praying for a lady troubled by spiritual problems. The woman had been 'set free' in a remarkable way; but, on the way home, her father turned to her and said,

'You know, everyone I pray for doesn't get delivered!' Why did he say that? She never asked. Perhaps he knew that his family may have felt a little over burdened by their father's apparent success.

With Martin Williams, John Valentine, Dave Wetherley and Bible School students in Zimbabwe.

Cage House revisited

CHAPTER 7
A FRUSTRATED PREACHER

AUCHENHEATH

Because he was travelling abroad frequently by the late '70s, G.W. began to consider another move. He thought it would be sensible if he and Dolly lived near to an international air terminal; it seemed obvious that they should be closer to Heathrow.

Instead, however, to the astonishment of their family, they responded to an invitation from Dr. Jack Kelly and his wife Eileen to make their home in Scotland. Their children wondered whether their parents had taken leave of their senses! But the family became less incredulous when they found that the place where their parents were going to settle was only twenty miles from Prestwick International air port and the same distance from a commuter airport.

Jack Kelly, a consultant heart surgeon at Paisley Royal Infirmary, had for some years been holding fellowship meetings at his home in Glasgow. These had always been held outside of church service times, Jack and Eileen not wishing to draw people away from their regular places of worship. In due course they had bought a large house with 28 acres of land at Auchenheath, near Lanark.

Although the couple had not initially been in favour of G.W.'s ministry, after Eileen had attended a conference in Liverpool at which G.W. had been the preacher, he was invited to Auchenheath to speak to the fellowship there. Regular preaching visits were followed by an invitation to the Norths to make their home at Auchenheath House [known as 'The Big Hoose' locally]. The Kellys and the Norths were to become firm friends.

So in 1977 they moved into the lodge on the Auchenheath estate; the second such lodge they had inhabited. This estate was on a much grander scale than the one at The Longcroft. The lodge itself was smaller and ideally suited to their needs. Did they feel that they had gone up in the world again? Did they look back to their origins and wonder? One young man in the Fellowship describes how he had overestimated the grandness of their arrival:

'When they arrived at Auchenheath I was very impressed by the amount of possessions they had, or rather didn't have. I had cleared a large area in the loft of the tractor garage to accommodate all their things while we finished painting and decorating the lodge; but I need not have bothered because the sum total of their worldly goods was: three tea chests, two cardboard boxes, two suitcases [bursting at the seams and tied together with a pair of old tights], two comfortable chairs and a standard lamp. I owned more than they did and I wasn't even married. They reminded me of the story in the Bible where the Shunnamite woman [2 Kings 4] gets her husband to build a room for the holy man of God on the roof of their house and she says, *Let us set for him there a bed, a table, a stool and a candlestick.* It was not very much that they were putting into the room, but apparently all that a holy man of God needed. It struck me as the same sort of thing and a great testimony to them both of not being concerned about worldly possessions.'

The house was in a lovely setting and soon became furnished with a few more worldly possessions. Jack took over G.W.'s itinerary arrangements, taking responsibility for getting him to his preaching engagements. G.W. did serve the Fellowship in the capacity of an elder and preacher, but spent much of his time abroad.

Now the children and grandchildren had to travel to Scotland for visits; but they loved the beautiful scenery and the generous Scottish hospitality. However, they did complain that the meetings were the longest they had ever sat through, which was saying something! But the lodge was good for holidays, especially Christmas ones, when, on Christmas Eve, Eileen and her helpers would put on a wonderful candlelit meal in the big house for at least twenty people.

Mickey Wright, one of the Auchenheath congregation at the time, says of his involvement with G.W. during his years of residence there :-

'I would describe the man I got to know over the next ten years as a man I could trust to tell me clearly, without any waffle, exactly where he stood on a matter and exactly what he believed to be right. He was a man who would stand by his convictions, no matter who would oppose him and no matter what the consequences.

Our church service included open worship and anyone was allowed to pray, start a hymn or chorus, prophesy, speak in tongues or share a word or testimony. This kind of service could leave you open to all sorts of things happening. Mr. North had an ability to keep them going in the direction he thought the Lord was leading, and was not afraid to stop someone if they were taking the meeting off in the wrong direction, and that included me. He did not let me off with anything at all; in fact I thought he was quite hard on me sometimes. His reply, after sorely reprimanding me for something, was very simply,

"I want you to be a man of God, Mick."

Once, after having been in Nigeria for several months I started a chorus which was a favourite with the Nigerians; *Let God arise and His enemies be scattered*. It was a very popular chorus and I had been singing it a lot. I had known the Lord for about four years at this time. We had only reached the second line when the chorus, which quite a few folks had taken up, came to a withering halt! I opened my eyes to see what had happened to find 'The General', as we secretly called him, waving his hands and shouting,

"No, no!" Then he asked us, as only he could,

"Why do you want to go back into the Old Covenant? God is risen beloved. He is risen! Hallelujah!" He then led us in a great shout of praise and the meeting took off again.

I had, however, been seriously injured by these proceedings and felt very rejected. The chorus I had chosen had been tossed away and I was upset. Mr. North then preached but I didn't hear a word of it as I struggled with my inner pain. The meeting came to an end, but I was still riveted to my seat. As Mr. North passed me on his way out, he lifted my chin and said,

"All right, Mick?"

"No!" was my resounding reply.

"Well, get right!" was his reply as he walked away. This was pain upon pain and I spent the rest of the evening brooding in the garden.

The following day, while repairing the drive, I saw Mr. North out walking and, joining him, launched into my complaint about his treatment of me the previous evening. Somehow or other, I ended up agreeing that it was all for my good. He had wanted to keep the meeting on track and I should not be in a huff about it, but be able to accept that it had to be done. He wanted me to be able to go through these things with a good attitude, even if they did smart a bit, so that I would be a man of God. He wanted me to go the same way he had gone and he didn't let himself off with anything either.

Mr. North was very supportive of us when my wife and I and baby daughter left the church in Auchenheath to go to Lanark to plant a new church. We were prayed for and sent out to Lanark with a £20 pound a week offering. In 1983 this was enough to buy a week's food. Mr. and Mrs. North faithfully gave us £5 per week out of their pension. I don't think their pension was very much at that time, but we could always rely on their support. Mrs. North also saved all her loose change and when it reached a reasonable amount she would put it into little purses she had collected from her travels and give it to our children.

We had wonderful fellowship. We didn't always agree, but we always parted friends. In all my years as a Christian I have never met anyone quite like Mr. North. I feel that I have been privileged to have known him. I have gleaned many precious insights into God's character and workings because of the wealth of his knowledge and understanding and also the wonderful revelations he had from God. I learned most of all, however, from watching him live. He was a flesh and blood example, in my generation of someone who was truly walking with God."

ZIMBABWE – AMEVA

During his years at Auchenheath, G.W.'s itinerary continued to expand to include Malaysia, Sicily, and perhaps most notably, Zimbabwe. Some of the leaves from the tree had fallen there in the form of John and Celia Valentine. True to form, GW. was a great encourager of the work there. Previously he had been to preach at John's invitation when John had been a missionary in Nigeria. Now G.W. enthusiastically took up the cause of Ameva Farm, as the place in Zimbabwe had been named.

'At Cliff Conference,' John reflects, 'he encouraged me to tell the people what my vision was for the work in Zimbabwe. He assured me that he would get behind me and felt that other people should do the same.

It was really because of this that the whole thing became a possibility.' G.W. gave the work a boost by taking up offerings, as well as publicising it by taking part in a promotional video.

John and Celia had gone from Liverpool fellowship in 1982, purchased an old tobacco farm near Chegutu in Northern Zimbabwe and set up an agricultural, chicken and cattle farm. On the farm they set up a Bible School, primary school and also a weaving shed. Later a secondary school was added to this work and a building known as The Straw Church. All this was in conjunction with the Christian Marching Church of Zimbabwe. The farm has a huge acreage and includes a compound for the workers and a dam which supplies all the area's water needs.

John tells how the first time that G.W. went to teach at the Bible School, 'he said,

"Give me one session" – there were four sessions every morning - . The next day he said,

"Give me two sessions." The next day it was three. The fourth day he wanted the whole morning! In the end he was doing all the teaching while he was there. In the evenings we'd have a general meeting, when everybody would come in, and that was wonderful, because he was really in his element. He loved that. They were tremendous times and I thank God for him because he was certainly an inspiration to me. He was my spiritual father. He had such a tremendous grasp of the Scriptures. Lots of people went out from the Bible School all over Africa. G.W. was instrumental in getting that work going.'

The Bible School at Ameva was run for five years by Martin Williams, G.W.'s son-in-law. He and his family moved from Solihull to work at the farm. Marian Williams helped with the teaching in the primary school and Bible School, at the same time providing hospitality for some of the many workers from various fellowships who were working temporarily on the compound.

After his 1993 visit to Ameva G.W. wrote an 'update' of his activities in which he reported:

'I was struck by the fact that over near the Kariba Dam among the Tonga tribe a great work is going on for God. These people were displaced from the valley in which the big Kariba Dam is storing up precious life-giving water for the people. These dear displaced people have received the Gospel, chiefly through the lips of two ex-students from Ameva. It is reported that there is almost a revival going on there, in that within twelve months or so some forty preaching stations have been set up and a large building holding about two hundred has been erected.

The work is so encouraging, not only to the people there, but to everyone who, by labour or by giving of their substance, has enabled it to proceed in the name of the Lord. Dear John [Valentine] was very blessed by it, saying,

"Man, it's like a Revival going on out there!" He intends to visit the place. They need encouragement; they need our prayers; they need what we can give them. What a wonderful opportunity!'

During a message preached in Warrington, G.W stated,

'Ameva farm and Bible School is one of the most wonderfully productive works I have visited in the world; it is an investment for God.' In the same message, in which he is appealing for workers for Zimbabwe, G.W. became rather scathing about people needing a 'call' before going to the mission field:

'The trouble with everybody is that they think they're very important. How many people in the Bible got a call? I don't think you'll be able to count to twenty. If you compile a list you'll find they were the very important people. Without saying so, or without thinking about it, you're saying, 'I'm very important!' Proof of this is that you think you must have a call like Paul or Elisha, or Hudson Taylor, or some other great man. Did you wait for a call to stay in England? God doesn't accept excuses. You and I are under a command. He said, "Go!" He did not say, "Wait for a call."'

It may be gathered from this that G.W. perhaps wished he were young again and able to go and work abroad, so great an impact did the work in Africa have on him.

'He loved teaching the students,' says John. It was indeed one of the great joys of his life to be able to have a part in the success of Ameva, which became a highly prosperous farm, as well as teaching centre, neighbouring farmers sometimes expressing a wish that they could send all their workers to Ameva schools. Although the work has suffered much during recent troubled times, it is still continuing, though sadly at a reduced pace.

PAINFUL LESSONS

As her husband's work began to include long spells – as much as six months – abroad, it was felt that Dolly should be moved into the big Auchenheath House. The lodge was, of course, near to the road and was isolated from the house by a drive. Sometimes Dolly's peace would be disturbed by local lads, who could be quite intimidating. So a large flat was prepared for her and Wally. It had lovely views over the garden, and with log fires burning in the grate, they must have felt like lords of the manor! Perhaps they marvelled at the transition from the East End of London and a bathroom-less overcrowded tiny country cottage to a mansion house.

It proved, indeed, a blessing that they were living in the larger community when, in 1984, Wally came down with a particularly painful bout of shingles. It was while he was preaching in the USA. that he came into contact with some children suffering from chickenpox and began to be ill. Fred Tomlinson travelled from Canada to take him back to their home. 'By that time,' says Fred, 'his face was raw with the shingles,' and they hastily arranged for his return to the U.K.

'That was the only occasion when Sheila and I were relieved to see Mr. North leave,' Fred remarks. 'He was like a father to Sheila and me and a kindly grandfather to our children.' This was the experience of many families with whom he stayed. People loved to have him in their homes and he was asked to marry numbers of young couples. Perhaps they thought that the knot would be better tied if G.W. tied it!

One Birmingham church leader, Ron Bailey, with whose large family G.W. and his wife loved to stay, claimed,

'One of the greatest joys of my life was to sit and talk with him. He told me God gave him a commission – "*Gather up the stones; lift up a standard for the people.* [Isaiah] People don't understand that when I'm on the platform, I have to lift up a standard for the people. God only ever commands what is perfect. He permits what is imperfect. From the platform I can only preach what is perfect."'

'He was two people,' says Ron. 'He was a herald and a pastor. When he first came to Birmingham and I was sitting in on his counselling sessions he was so gentle, he was like a nursing mother with a baby. People didn't see that on the platform. You saw this man with a sword in his hand, and there was no compromise, but when this man was counselling people, he was so gentle; so patient.

Particularly after his illness [shingles] when he did less counselling, the only side you ever saw of him was the man with a sword in his hand. For some people it was difficult. If they only knew that man I can understand why they didn't take to him; but if they knew the man that came into your house and saw him with your children....!'

Indeed, G.W.'s illness, coming as it did when he was aged 70, did make a marked difference to his future ministry. The shingles was of the rarer kind, attacking him in the head, making his skin and the inside of his ears, nose and throat extremely painful and raw. He couldn't bear to wash his face or shave his beard, a most distressing thing for one who liked to look immaculate. He couldn't speak properly for many months and didn't want to see anyone.

At first, his daughters, when phoning to enquire after their father were told by their mother not to visit yet as he could not speak to them and it was no use coming to see him. When they did come, after he was a little better, they could not take the children to see him or give their father a hug and kiss. That would have been too painful for him.

One remarkable thing that did happen during his illness was that, having resisted it for so long, mainly because Dolly was adamant, Wally was glad to be presented with a television. The family had got together and decided that a T.V. would be the best thing to distract their father from his intense pain. So his son-in-law Nicholas put a large set in the car and drove up to Auchenheath, wondering whether he would have to take it home again. But it was gratefully received. Now the patient was able to watch cricket etc. when he was unable to do anything else; even reading or listening to music were out of the question. His wife became an avid snooker addict!

As a result of the shingles, having been a music lover all his life, G.W. could not now take any pleasure in listening to it. For ever afterwards he found it very difficult to sit through the early part of meetings where singing was going on. When he was preaching he had to come on just before the sermon. Perhaps it looked as though he was making a grand entrance, in the manner of some preachers, but this was just the way the illness affected him.

The pain remained in some measure for the rest of G.W.'s life. Big hugs were too uncomfortable to welcome any more, so he may have seemed stand-offish. Having been a strong and healthy person most of his life, he confessed that he now had had, 'a glimpse of what others must have gone through in their day.' The thing that he seemed most grateful for during his illness was the love shown to him by other people. Writing to the Fellowships in November 1984, he says,

'You will, I presume, have heard of the Lord's ministry to me in the U.S.A. and Canada in days of great pain, how that love abounded toward me and hearts and homes were opened to me so that I had need of nothing. None could have been kinder to me and more patient and gentle than they. And their generosity matched their love, so that in sickness I discovered the preciousness of love in a way that strength and health knows nothing of, for it has no need.'

Later in this letter he says,

'I am not yet free of pain, though better than I was. I have a beard, I have a song in my heart, my spirit is up, the Lord is good!'

In a further letter, dated 12th January 1985, G.W. speaks of all the cards, letters and gifts 'that have poured in from all over the world' and of the, 'debt of gratitude' he owes his 'beloved brothers and sisters'.

'It leaves us profoundly grateful,' he writes, 'for being members of such a large family. It seems to stretch world-wide. How glorious that is! And I do trust that through it all our Father shall be glorified. If pain and suffering and illness make this contribution to a family, then it will be worth it all.'

Three months into his illness, G.W. admits,

'The progress I have made has been very, very slow; sometimes so minimal that I couldn't even see it over the space of a week.' In this "bulletin" he reports,

'I am using this method of dictation through the kindness of Dot [friend and tape secretary], who manages somehow to decipher what I can scarcely speak, for my speech organs have been affected and the muscles are only slowly [it seems to me very slowly, God give me patience,] returning to their former powers.'

He speaks in this letter of 'the unstinted labours of my wife', in answering the many letters he received, and of being 'taught dependence on others'.

After six months, during which he never left the house, G.W. sent out a final 'bulletin' to say that he, although not yet free of pain and not 'fully restored' was finding that his illness was now bearable and attacks were far less frequent. His main cause for rejoicing seems to have been that, 'The speech defect is well-nigh eliminated.' He could now sing a little and had been able to go into some prayer meetings for a short while.

It does seem to have worried him that he had been forced to send out 'bulletins', thinking that they might make him seem too important:-

'I am sorry to be sending these letters in one sense – in that I don't get circular letters from everybody else that's been ill, and I want you to know that I don't think that I'm any better than any of you, my precious brothers and sisters – it's just that so many of you have proved yourselves better than me, in that you have joined in and done all the lovely things that you've done towards me, which I have not done for you – and I want to say thank you ever so much. God's everlasting goodness to me has not only been extended by His Spirit but by many brothers and sisters as well....and for this I shall never be able to thank Him enough.'

It did worry him, perhaps unnecessarily, that he had been forced to cancel his preaching arrangements over the months he had been ill. 'Please forgive me,' was his plea to 'those who love me enough to be disappointed that I have not been able to fulfil my engagements with them; the loss is mine.' And in the final letter he shows his eagerness to be getting on with the work – no thoughts of retirement with him; though he admits, 'I don't quite know how to handle the future at the moment. I do not wish any of you to feel that I am neglecting you. I will try to give what I owe if you count me to be indebted.'

One of his daughters, after his illness, asked her father whether he thought he would ever again have the confidence to face preaching at big meetings, such as the Rora conference sessions. 'I don't know,' he told her. His speech was still a little affected.

However, in the letter dated 13th March 1985, he was urging himself and his 'brothers and sisters':-

'Let us, beloved, labour, shall we? Let us renew and, where it is possible, redouble our efforts to serve the Lord and spread the glorious news, and be to others what they need as well as give to God all that is His.' One member of the Fellowship at Eltham, London, remembers that, though G.W. was booked to speak at their Easter conference, the congregation were not sure whether he would turn up or not after his long illness.

'When I saw him,' she said, 'he looked very frail and I wondered whether he would be able to carry on. But as he preached he seemed to get stronger and stronger and my thoughts then were,

"It's amazing what the Spirit can do!"

Man at work at Auchenheath

CHAPTER 8
AN AGEING PREACHER

BRACKNELL AND BEYOND

Though G.W. did continue to travel extensively at home and abroad his family began to think that perhaps their parents should be living somewhere nearer to one of their daughters. As their youngest daughter Carole and her family were living in Bracknell, near to Heathrow, they decided in 1989 to settle there. The church was eager to include them in the Fellowship and have the benefit of G.W.'s ministry when he was at home.

The problem of finding a home for the now fairly elderly couple was resolved by a family friend offering to buy a flat in which they could live for as long as they liked. Though it would never belong to them, this idea suited them. They had never wanted to be property owners and saw this generous offer as God's provision, as indeed it was, for the whole family as well as for the couple themselves. A lovely flat was found, only five minutes' walk away from their daughter and the local shops. The church people helped to prepare it for them and they were delighted to move into it, though greatly missing their Scottish home.

Now Dolly could become a 'normal' housewife again. It was quite daunting for her after ten years living in a place isolated from the shops and being able to join the folks in the big house for meals when she didn't feel like cooking. But she and Wally soon settled into a new routine, taking frequent walks to the shops and living a bit more of a private life. Conveniently, when at home, they were able to walk down to visit their daughter's family on an almost daily basis, though Wally was still often away and sometimes took his wife with him.

Many evenings were spent by Dolly trying to beat her husband and their friend Celia at Scrabble. Much to Dolly's disgust, he nearly always won! She and Celia thought he cheated, making up some rare words, but it was her ambition to claim a victory. It happened occasionally.

Interestingly, after Dolly's death, her husband would never play Scrabble again, claiming, to the surprise of his family, that he couldn't stand the game and had only played it so often in order to please his wife.

Dolly threw herself into the life of the church and faithfully supported it for the rest of her life, never liking to miss meetings if she could possibly get to them. At one point, following a crisis in the church, G.W. briefly took over the pastorship and astonished everyone by his ability to take up the reigns of responsibility again. The crisis, which involved his own family, worried Dolly; she thought it might hinder her husband's ministry; but it has been observed since that it has had just the opposite effect; endearing people to the preacher.

GOLDEN WEDDING

It was in Bracknell in 1991 that Wally and Dolly celebrated fifty years of married life, the church putting on a marvellous party for them. The Fellowship people collected information for a 'This is your Life' red book, and, as on the T.V. programme, big surprises were in store.

In a gathering of old friends and relatives, Dolly produced from her handbag, which she hadn't let out of her sight all day, the first 'love-letter', as she called it, which Wally had sent her over fifty years ago. Even her husband had not realised she had kept it. She also, of course, had kept his letters from Maidstone prison, quoted earlier in this story.

The arrival of Wally's sister and brother-in-law from Australia at the appropriate moment was greeted with shouts of joy. But the best surprise of all was the unexpected appearance of their daughter Marian from Zimbabwe. None of the family knew this was going to happen; the excitement ran high.

One of the tape messages sent for this wonderful day - -even the weather was glorious – included some observations about G.W. :-

G.W.N. , after speaking for about an hour, always put his spectacles into the top pocket of his suit jacket, saying,

'I suppose I'd better finish,' and then carried on for fifteen minutes!

In his heart he seems to have Quaker doctrine, Methodist romance, Holiness living, Salvation Army fire, Pentecostal fervour and Brethren discipline.

An Ageing Preacher

About 25 years ago, G.W. announced in a meeting,

'I've asked the Lord for another 25 years and I believe I've got them.'

He was right!

Dolly's panacea for every cut and bruise was Germolene. Perhaps that explains why G.W.N. always manages to collect innumerable lotions, creams etc. for every minor ailment, from every hostess, from every place where he stays.

At the end of the red book someone has written about Dolly,

'Mrs. North; someone once prayed for her for grace to be married to "that man". She told them that it really wasn't that bad. But it must take some woman to endure the following:-

We conservatively reckon that she has sat in 14300 meetings for about 42900 hours i.e. one long meeting of about 4.9 years with 'my beloved' speaking for about 17875 hours i.e. one long preach of about 2.04 years!'

Though this was a truly wonderful day, Dolly's health had been deteriorating. She had never believed in going to the doctor's, and both of them had been treated, when necessary, by medical practitioners whom they met whilst travelling or who were resident in their home Fellowships. It was difficult for the family to persuade her to see a doctor, though she had grown very thin, having been quite a large woman during her fifties and sixties.

She would not hear of her husband's staying at home to look after her. His work was her priority as well as his and she knew he would not have been happy without doing it. Their eldest daughter was now living nearby with her husband and children, so G.W., although hesitant, was able to go, knowing his wife would be well looked after by the church as well as the family.

Dolly did make one last trip to Cyprus in 1993, accompanied by her daughter and Celia, a close friend, to help look after her. However, she did find the trip extremely tiring and G.W. admitted, on his return, that he wished he had not taken her, though this had been a favourite destination for them both.

FAREWELL TO DOLLY

_ In the same year as the Cyprus trip [1993] G.W. celebrated his 80th Birthday. Some of his old friends arranged a holiday in the Lake District with family and friends. During that week a big party was thrown in his honour. The following year it was Dolly's turn to celebrate turning 80. Her party was much smaller, held at their home and given by family and church friends. She wanted to invite all the older people in the church, including those who were sometimes left out of such events. This was a very happy occasion, especially as her beloved husband was at home to share in the festivities.

The couple were now living in a newly fitted out spacious ground floor flat with a large garden. This had been lovingly provided for them by a church member, a business man who owned several properties in the area and had felt that the Lord had told him to provide a home for the Norths. The need for them to move had become apparent when Dolly was finding difficulty in managing the steps up to their previous flat.

She was delighted to have a garden again, primarily so that she could hang the washing outside! Her husband, however, found himself spending many hours toiling in the garden. But he was still strong and hearty and he did have some help. He would say, after his wife died,

'I did it for Dolly.' And it was indeed a labour of love; he did not relish all the hard work. He was able to give up his toil when the garden was landscaped by the owner and planted out beautifully, largely with roses, which were Dolly's favourite flowers.

She was, however, to have only six months in her new home. G.W. was planning a preaching trip to Canada, accompanied by his youngest daughter. Carole, now on her own, had been travelling with her father, and looking after his itinerary for several years, [though he would sometimes say, 'I'm looking after her!'].

G.W. was concerned about his wife's health and wondering whether he should leave her. But she urged him to continue with his work, saying that she would be alright with plenty of people to keep an eye on her. She wouldn't hear of his giving up preaching unless absolutely necessary. Wasn't the Lord looking after her? Besides, the owner of their flat had installed in the upstairs flat a younger church member, who would be on call if needed.

This time it did turn out to be needed and G.W., now in Canada, had to be called to say that his wife was in hospital. Of course, immediate arrangements were made for his return; but before that, his hostess at the time remembers that he prayed,

'We are not happy about this, Lord, but our hearts are full of joy,' and with that, went calmly upstairs for a nap.

On his return to the U.K., he found that Dolly was not in pain and was able to talk to him. The doctors were offering to amputate her leg to save her life; but this had to be a family decision. The idea was too shocking to contemplate; but the father and two daughters, with one of Dolly's grandsons, repaired to the café to discuss the daunting prospect before them; the daughters offering to look after their mother if Dad wanted to permit the operation. Feeling rather dazed, they decided to go to the hospital chapel and pray for God's help. On coming out of the chapel, they found the surgeon looking for them, to tell them that the patient had now reached a condition where an operation would not save her. They thanked God that they had not had to make this impossible choice.

Dolly's grandchildren now gathered and all were able to say goodbye to a conscious, but thankfully pain free grandmother. Most of them were standing round her bed with their parents when she died peacefully and were able to join in singing her favourite hymns. When she had first seen her husband, two days before she passed away, she had asked him to bring her a rose from the garden, telling him that it was better for her to go than for him, because he could carry on preaching the Gospel. What better wife could a preacher have had? He took the rose to her funeral. Many gathered to pay tribute to her life, one person perhaps summing it up by saying,

'She was the perfect wife for him. She brought him down to earth.'

This was so; Norman described her as 'a very homely woman.' It had not been an easy life for a poorly educated country girl, taken out of her comfort zone and transported into a supporting role for a wide-ranging ministry. But it was her very simplicity that endeared her to all who knew her.

'I was not worthy of her,' her husband said.

A short time after his wife's funeral G.W. was preaching at the couple's old home, The Longcroft, and shared with the people there,

'You will know that not long ago dear Dolly went to be with the Lord. I don't know whether you were there round the grave. I couldn't stand it any longer and I started singing, *Thine be the glory*. The proper place to dance and shout Hallelujah is round a grave. Did you know that?'

Though he and the congregation had certainly been in triumphant mood at her memorial service, G.W. was lost without his wife. He could somehow not bring himself to do any more writing, though he often tried, taking up his writing materials many times to continue his work. But for some reason the inspiration wouldn't come.

LIFE AFTER DOLLY

It was obvious that G.W., now aged 81, couldn't live by himself. Coming from a generation where men were totally looked after domestically by their wives, he was at a loss. Though his daughters tried to look after him in his own home for six months, his upstairs neighbour was horrified one day to smell burning and find a dried up pan on the cooker.

His eldest daughter Judith, with her husband and younger daughter, decided that she had to move into her father's spacious home to look after him. The house was very convenient for this, as they were able to occupy both the upstairs and downstairs flats. God had provided for them in their need, as G.W. had expected Him to do. This was the way he and his wife had always lived and they had never been forsaken.

G.W.'s ministry continued around the UK.; but, about a year after Dolly's death, whilst on a preaching engagement in Worthing, he suffered a minor stroke and was brought home for assessment, treatment and recuperation. His speech was very slightly affected, but after a while and many miles of walking with his daughter for exercise, he was making a good recovery.

As he had been advised not to do any preaching for six months, he felt at a loose end and began to think about visiting his sister and brother-in-law in Australia .His nieces were urging him to go and promising to look after him along with their parents; a promise carried out with great generosity, energy and warmth.

BEING A PREACHER

Although most appreciative of all the love showered upon him in Sydney, it is revealing of G.W.'s state of mind at the time that he says in a journal he kept whilst there:

'The biggest disappointment of all to me is the entire cessation from preaching that this visit to Australia imposes upon me. Preaching and writing books, articles etc. has so filled my life these many years that I find cessation from it a major adjustment; but God gives more grace than any situation and occupation can demand, and I am still a pupil. *Lord teach me to number my days that I may apply my heart unto wisdom.*' [Text for the day]

Apart from during a few days when in India, this was the only time in his life that G.W. had kept a diary. Somebody had presented him with a set of journals with Scripture texts on each page, asking him to record his comments on the texts each day. This request he tried to follow, though the texts are repeated several times throughout one of the books. Some of the extracts from this diary are worth repeating here. For instance:-

October 3rd '95 The text for today has registered strongly with me *[The words that I speak unto you are spirit and they are life. John 6: 13].* Life has to be maintained. Words spoken are spirit and life. Only Christ's words are eternal life, but all words, of whatever intention, or meaning, have the life of the speaker in them. Lord, forever keep this fact before me, that my lips may always be praiseworthy in Thy sight; lest words of mine should turn aside some soul or souls and I displease Thee. I am aware many have been affected by what I have said through the years. The responsibility of a preacher is terrible and insupportable except *all his ways are pleasantness and all his paths are peace.* God be my way and also my life.

This diary entry ties up with an article G.W. had written some years previously, in which he had expressed his beliefs about his own profession:-

'The awful responsibility of being a preacher lies heavily upon me this morning.....A preacher is of necessity a man of words.....How absolutely vital it is that preachers preach the word of God and not their own word. If they do not, faith will not come to a man's heart; if that does not happen he cannot be saved. The responsibility for men's salvation lies, in part, on the shoulders of the preacher; the preacher <u>must</u> realise this. Not <u>all</u> the responsibility, but a great deal of it. The complete responsibility is shared between three parties – God; the person to be saved; the preacher.

God, who provided salvation, is the Saviour; His is the greatest part. The person to be saved must be operative also; he must believe. The person to be saved <u>must</u> hear the word of God. Behold, then, the work of the preacher – he is the link between God and the unsaved man.

The preacher must therefore realise that:-

He is the one held responsible by God to bring the word of God to that person.

What he speaks must be the word of God.

It must be the word of faith.

It must be the word of power.'

He then goes on to list the responsibilities of the listener, but says that this cannot be made an excuse for negligence on the part of the preacher.

He continues:-

'The preacher must not think that words <u>about</u> God are the word of God or that the Bible is the Word of God and all he has to do is preach a sermon and hope that God will 'use' it.

The preacher must not fall prey to church jargon – ' giving a message, giving a word' and similar phrases much in use. Paul's instruction to Timothy must be taken to heart – *'Preach the word'* [2 Timothy 4] meaning he must speak as God is speaking.

True preaching is prophetic, i.e. The preacher must know he is indwelt by the Spirit of prophecy and know that he is being used by God.'

Is it any wonder he was such a powerful preacher? And would these words be enough to deter other would be preachers?

THE DIARY.

Sunday. 8-10-95 I have not found it easy to adjust to going to gather with God's people when I am not leading and preaching to them. I do so at home [in Bracknell], but elsewhere I do not fit in. I do hope that it is only due to physical and not spiritual and psychological reasons. It is perilously easy to insist on being the central figure or else, if this is not granted, stay away altogether. O God, in these latter days of my life, keep me from pride. Help me always to remember Lucifer's sin and punishment, and to never forget the accusation against the Ephesians – *'Thou hast left thy first love – thou hast fallen.'* - Let Thy angels bear me up, O Lord.

I am so grateful to Thee for all Thou hast done for me and been to me. If I have not been as appreciative as I ought, or presumed beyond propriety, please forgive me. If I have misused or abused my position and powers, please forgive me and cleanse me. Let not Thy perfections and my imperfections create distance between us.

If I have failed [and I am sure I have; perhaps I ought to say to what degree I have failed] and disappointed Thy hope, O Lord, please forgive me. Is the missed opportunity a lost opportunity? Art Thou disappointed in me, Lord? Blot out of my memory the things wherein I have failed Thee, lest torment plague me and shortcoming be the sad story of my life. Oh, that I may fulfil the hope of Thy heart for me! It's late in life for me. I do not wish for the gay abandon of youth, nor do I want to exist in the carnality of old age; seeking to dress up my soul with false promises.

Wash me clean, O Lord. May I fulfil Thy hope. This is my hope. So many speak of the hope of His return. This is a valid hope, but it is a certainty also. Surely the hope of all hopes is fulfilling God's hope.

Mon. 23-10-95 It is a strange feeling to meet every day with the sense of having nothing to do. The oft-stated reprimand [loving, of course] of the family to 'do nothing' or 'go steady' is very prohibitive and limiting. Days drag. Reading has increased to the point where I do not wish to read. Both sight and hearing are impaired also. So, with decreasing strength deterring me, I am not fitting in to the 'no function' bracket notably well; but the Lord is good and I must continue to ' lay up treasure in Heaven' [Text for the day: - *'For where your treasure is there your heart will be also'* Matthew 6:21]

Mon. 23-10-95 Rene says that she is a 'this end of the day person' and Alf is a 'that end of the day person' – such is life!

Tues. 24-10-95 We were late abed last evening; a man named J. called around and stayed an hour or so, talking mostly of church matters and his view of the Scriptures etc. It all finished with him dropping on his knees and asking us to pray for him, which we did. He seems a self-effacing man, for he constantly excused himself for thinking and saying what he did. There was no need for such a negation of self. It seems he has a great respect for age. He is a nice man.

Wed. 25-10-95   We spent a long time this morning over Bible reading and prayer, and are very blessed. The chapter was 1 Corinthians 13. We lingered long in prayer. O, Lord enable me to live consciously in this love, daily putting away babyhood and child hood to become a man. I need a sword; not a drumstick; love, not sentimentality. I do not want dolls and teddy bears and rocking-horses. I am a man. I do not want to talk baby talk and call Thee Abba all my life. I want to call Thee Father.

There is much to save us from; not the least of which is the untaught and underfed mind.

Friday 27-10-95   I have found this to be a chilly Spring. Summer, I am told, commences in November. I look forward to it! Australian houses are cold. Central heating is unknown. I miss it very much. Rene is a fresh air fanatic. Doors and windows have to be open; and quite frequently she goes out of the house in her night attire and walks and sits around while I am sitting with an electric fire in front of me!

Sat. 28-10-95   Yesterday I received letters from home enclosing cheque from the conference. Thank you Lord! Felt mildly reproved because during conversation yesterday I had mentioned money, saying that my reserves were running low; a most unusual thing for me to do. Thank you, Lord for your tender ways with me – too gentle, I feel, at times. Lord, do not let my heart become wayward, nor let my tongue become the instrument of discontent. I remember that of old you overthrew your redeemed people because they murmured against you and your ways. Thou, my God of all abundance, will supply my need. Even as the day is now springing in the East, it testifies of your faithfulness. I love Thee. Wash me and cleanse my heart from sin.

Mon-30-10-95   It seems that no revival or move of the Spirit ever has, or ever will accomplish the Herculean task of breaking the denominational hold. It's a folly of man that they must be able to give everything a name.

Tues. 1-11-95 Rene is very active; still full of energy, sharp of wit, repartee unimpaired, uncomplaining. She waddles determinedly, swaying from side to side, naps now and then, usually not for long, cooks, washes, sews busily with machine and needle. Her sight is remarkable and her eye is bright. She extols God frequently, bursting into snatches of song, sometimes tunelessly, but nevertheless acceptable to God; expressing praise and thanks and love. I cannot recall a day since I have been here that she has not blessed the Lord and in doing so has blessed me, and I frequently join her in a hymn or chorus we learned in childhood. Alf too sings, his taste being in C.of E. tunes and hymns, they too being stored up since childhood. He retains his eldership at the 'Foursquare' church in Sydney, to which they both go on Sundays. I go nowhere except to preach, and at times castigate myself for it, but the Lord knows the thoughts and intents of my heart. Perhaps the cacophony of sounds in my head [since having shingles] will one day depart and congregational singing will again be enjoyable to me.

Friday. 4-11-95 Yesterday we suffered a sudden and devastating squall; a terrific wind accompanied by thunder, lightening, rain and hail. It ripped in on us. While we were struggling to shut doors and windows in one room the rain was sweeping into another, soaking the bedding. It lasted about ten minutes; but the violence of it will live in my memory for a long while. Uncontrollable nature is frightening.

Sat. 5-11-95. Australia is in process of the run up to the election. Voting is compulsory, which I find objectionable. Votes need to be won, not commanded; punishment for abstention from voting is a contradiction of civil liberties, so highly extolled. Having never voted all my life, I find it strange that Christians partake in politics. He who votes must partake of the laws made by the party of his choice; good or evil, beneficial or otherwise. Theocracy and Democracy are totally opposed.

Sat 11-11-95 [Text for the day: *Draw near to God and He will draw near to you.* James 4:8] Luther called this epistle [James] 'an epistle of straw' and not without reason, I suggest. I must confess that I have my doubts about its inclusion in the N.T. I am very glad that it is agreed that it was not written by the apostle James; each of the apostles was an apostle of Jesus Christ. That a born again man could write a work of Scriptural importance and not speak of Jesus specifically and pivotally is amazing. He speaks of the synagogue and of religion and gives good advice, mentions the Devil and healing; but hardly mentions Jesus. Why?

Tues. 21-11-95.[Text for the day: *And all things, whatsoever you ask in prayer believing, you will receive.* Matthew 21:22]. This should cause all of us much thought. I cannot say I have received all I have ever asked for from the Lord. So much He has given without my asking that I have ceased to ask. Some aspects of prayer mystify me. To differentiate between what I should ask for and what I should not ask for seems a fundamental thing, I think. To be convinced I shall receive if I ask is a basic principle, I am sure. Without this it is better not to ask. Certainty is fundamental to prayer, lest requests become vain repetitions.

Friday. 1-12-95.   The point which arose in conversation was: 'Should a person who has been overtaken in a fault and has repented, and has sought restitution and acceptance and is apparently turned from his sin be accepted among the saints again, and be allowed to minister?' I say yes. I have recalled that Dr. Smellie, of some standing in Christian circles, said, 'Rather than let love suffer, let truth suffer.' What Jesus said about the Father in the parable of the Prodigal Son lies deep in my heart. He has done this for me. Let me do it for others.

Breaking into the diary here to quote from one of the Fellowship leaders:

'He [G.W.] always erred on the side of love.'

At one time some of the Fellowship elders were displeased with a certain preacher in their midst and were calling for discipline. One of their number remembers G.W. saying, *Deal kindly with the young man for my sake* [Quoting from King David's example towards his rebellious son, Absalom]. This had an effect on fellowship elders' actions when dealing with such disciplinary matters. Indeed G.W. did go to some extreme measures in order to 'deal kindly' with any who had erred, sometimes many feeling that he went too far in that direction, seemingly forgetting those who had been wronged. Love was always in his mind – not confrontation. Some people found this frustrating.

G.W. sometimes used to quote from an old hymn by John Goss, first published in 1871,to explain his attitude:-

> *Was there ever kindest shepherd,*
> *Half so gentle, half so sweet*
> *As the Saviour, who would have us*
> *Come and gather round His feet.*

There's a wideness in God's mercy
Like the wideness of the sea.
There's a kindness in His justice
Which is more than liberty.

For the love of God is broader
Than the measure of man's mind,
And the heart of the Eternal
Is most wonderfully kind.

He always addressed congregations by calling them 'Beloved'.

Mon. 11-12-95. Yesterday there was torrential rain with thunder. Everyone seems to think that this Spring {and Summer so far} are uncharacteristic, being colder and wetter and more overcast than they can remember. The atomic explosions are blamed for it; the villains of the piece being the French. This may be true. There have been international protests but they have ignored them and, judging on balance, who can blame them?

Those nations that condemn them have already carried out the kind of tests for which France is being criticised! To be in this world, but not of it, as the Lord Jesus prayed, should be taken as a rule of life for all of God's children. Though indirectly, even to vote in this world's systems involves a person in the politics of war, death and destruction.

Wed. 13-12-95. [Text from James]. I find James enigmatic and read him hesitantly; he seems to make no distinction between Israel and the Church and frankly addresses his letter to the twelve tribes. This being so, I exclude myself from the company addressed, but benefit from what he says as from what Old Testament prophets said.

Sometimes the phraseology of ministers concerns me. For instance, as when a man says 'let us draw near to God in prayer,' as though hitherto he and his congregation have, until then, been away from God. I prefer Paul, who says, '*We who sometime were afar off are made nigh by the blood of Christ.*'

Friday. 29-12-95. Alf went fishing last evening and caught nothing. It is a long time now since I have 'caught' anything for the Lord. This inactivity imposed upon me by circumstances {bodily} is very irksome. I have a restlessness within me – I want to further invest what talent{s} pound{s} and gift{s} God has given – entrusted – to me. Preaching and /

or writing have been my occupation for so long now that to be kept from them is to be robbed of life itself. I do not rebel against God's will, but the sudden change from active ministry to doing nothing is a great loss to me. I had not anticipated it. Whether or not God has chosen to let me continue in this mode I do not know; what I do know is that His grace is sufficient for every one of His children.

Sat. 30-12-95. The Christmas hols. Have been an extravaganza of money, spending, eating, wine-bibbing, listening to Kiri T. singing Carols etc. Rene has sat doing puzzles. A test match has been on and we have watched that. I have been indulged a bit on that, watching it with Alf.

Mon 1-1-96. Yesterday I went to lunch with Lorna and D.. Marian{daughter} and Martin and Joanna were there also. We had an enjoyable time. Marian and Martin discussed their future with me. What they will do I do not know.

   I do so clearly remember the command of God to me – '*Go, and the Lord be with thee.*' It rings in my mind now as I write, and the excitement and joy of it possesses me afresh. The Lord has never withdrawn that command nor lessened the urge and urgency of it. He has never told me to cease from going nor said, 'Rest a while' and, as this year opens, the call and command is as lively in my soul as it has ever been. I do not want to use this ageing body as an excuse.

Tues. 2-1-96. Posted letters yesterday to Charlie C., who has suffered the loss of Mary, his wife. He addresses me as 'Dad'. He is the only one outside of the family who does so, and therefore holds a special place.

Friday 5-1-96. Yesterday I was able to do a little writing. I found it laborious, disappointingly so. Mental fluency and spelling correctness seem to have deserted me. I even stumble at reading. All is in the Lord's hands.

Sunday 7-1-96. Last night we reminisced about Edwin Taylor and his wife and the early days of Dunks Green. We went to bed very thankful to the Lord for having met and been under the influence of them both. They instilled in me so much.

Mon. 8-1-96. Marian and Martin with Joanna departed today for Malawi. It has been precious to see them again.

Sun. 14-1-96. I praise the Lord for the feeling of well-being that I have these days. He is so good to me. I thank Him with much feeling.

Mon. 15-1-96. Today I fly to Perth in the will of God to attempt to preach again there. It is some months since I last preached and I long to be able to do so again. It has been difficult and unusual to turn down invitations to preach, but I felt I should respond to Bernard's invitation to do so. As the Lord grants me the ability to do so I intend to take up my calling again, though I little thought it would be in Perth.

Tues. 16-1-96. D.V. I shall take my first meeting and look forward to it with a good deal of trepidation and yet joy. There is a degree of uncertainty in it for I have not addressed a meeting since Sept. 95.

Wed. 17-1-96. Temperature yesterday about 100 degrees. Last evening I spoke to a company of 50-60 persons of all ages. It was a great time. It is my first preachment for 4-5 months and it was good to be back in harness again – most blessed and enjoyable. I am looking forward to Friday when, if God will, I expect to be speaking again. I was very tired last evening and when I got up this a.m. felt stiff in every joint. I am still weary and finding it almost too great a task to write and to comment on the text for today.

Sat. 20-1-96 Today is relaxation day. I suppose I shall watch some tennis and little else beyond that. Above all, I hope to become fully prepared for tomorrow's meeting. Last evening many responded to the ministry.

Sun. 21-1-96. To preach I know I am sent. Let the power and authority of that sending be manifest this day, that the reason I am here and the purpose of Thy heart in this place may be accomplished, O Lord.

Wed. 24-1-96. Daily, as I pick up my lap-board to write, I am filled with gratitude to Bernard. He has refurbished it for me, replacing the tape which Fred T. stuck round the edges. I thank God who has provided me with such younger brothers as these, who it seems can hardly cease from doing me such favours.

Sat. 27-1-96. Yesterday was Australia Day and no-one was allowed to be unaware of it! Flags were waving everywhere; there were gatherings, singing, dancing, speech-making, barbecues – a public holiday. I heard and saw no reference to God, only nationalism; the great god, Australia! I think this must be the most vulgar, intolerant, Godless society in the world!

Tues. 13-2-06 Rose at 5.30. A good night. I feel rested. I have several letters to write but feel indisposed to do so. Have I overslept? The inner drive to write has deserted me. Perhaps it's only a temporary malaise. This country is in the grip of election fever- -parliamentarians are in the hustings. As in every democratic country, the unions rule. In the British Isles, the power of the unions, which was broken by the redoubtable Mrs. Thatcher, is gradually asserting itself.

'The good life' is a phrase frequently used. There is only one good life – the life of Jesus Christ. Self-denial is nowadays a word seldom heard in the pulpit, being sedulously avoided by preachers. Instead, prosperity and self-indulgence are deliberately substituted as being God's will for today.

Sun. 18-2-96. Rose at 2.40 that I might prepare my soul for preaching today at Essington.

p.m. This has been a great day. I preached from Luke 14+15 and the word was received with joy. It seemed that the Lord had worked in hearts. We came home with an invitation to return in March, which I gladly accepted.

Mon. 19-2-96. Fond remembrances of yesterday fill my mind. I am a bit weary with the exertions of preaching after not doing it for so long. I suppose I must expect some sort of tiredness as muscles and movements long neglected come into use again. I thank the Lord that of His mercy and grace I am able once more to engage in my calling.

Wed. 21-2 96. Went shopping yesterday. Alf is an avid shopper. He inspects nearly everything, taking up time and wearing himself out. Rene is rather more liberal. I push the trolley.

Matthew 3. Jesus was first called a Nazarene, like every other Nazarene. He was inconspicuous; there was nothing special about him. He had neither done nor said anything noteworthy.

John preached a spiritual baptism of repentance – he practised baptism in water. It is fatal to confuse the two. Water baptism cannot wash away sins – it is only a figure.

Friday. 23-2-96. Today we are expecting to go out to lunch with M. and N.

Matthew 5. Jesus set about laying down laws for His subjects. He was clearly God's emissary. He never touched on politics and the law of the land, but taught His hearers to obey it. His teachings were utterly spiritual and entirely pure and pacifist. Much was expected of the nation that had Him for their king.

Sunday. 25-2-96. Matthew 6. It is an amazing thing that, having read this book and this chapter many times, so much so that I am able to repeat its teaching and its very words from memory, I should reap benefit from it still and yet again learn something new. This New Testament of God's and ours is perennially fresh and its words ever new. I thank God for this treasury of love which is called the New Testament.

Sat. 2-3-96. Today is polling day. Lorna [niece] has said that she and Derrick will take Alf and Rene to the booth in their new car. Voting is compulsory for all Australian people. I am very glad that this is not the law in England; if it was I would be in gaol, for I have never voted – not once. I believe that I am in this world, but not of it, as the Lord Jesus said, and I have 'come out from among' the world's ideology and policy. Whatever country it is, whatever its political beliefs, be they good or bad, I am commanded to 'touch not the unclean thing'. I want to be an obedient child of God and He will then be to me a Father as he wants to be.

Tues. 5-3-96 Today I go to Hornsby to hairdressers. I wish to look at shoes. I regret buying the pair of shoes at Rhoda's last year. I found them too heavy. I do not wish to displease the Lord by wasting His money, so I know He will lead aright in what I want to do.

The last visit to the doctor's with Alf – I heard him say that he had Hodgkins Lymphoma, which I believe is a form of cancer. Having been informed by the girls that neither Alf nor Rene know the seriousness of the illness, I felt I could not tell Rene what I had heard at the doctor's. But, talking with her, I discovered that she was quite prepared for him to go. I spoke to her then of my expectations for Alf's health; but did not tell her of the doctor's words. Preoccupation with death does not make for pleasantness, but it seemed to me that Alf's early demise did not depress her and that she had 'given him up to God' some time ago.

Wed. 6-3-96. Rose at 3:30. Slept well. Thank you, Lord!

Went to Hornsby yesterday – to find some shoes. Both black and brown pairs are looking shabby. The brown pair I have had for some ten or more years. Both have served me well.

The {new} shoes are light but strong and though I have not worn them they please me well. God is wonderfully good to me.

I have mislaid my C.V. [cardio-vascular] tablets, but have no worries about them. I have been reducing the dose and am not wanting them today at all. It is my intention to further reduce them to one every other day in the future. Beside these I take one vitamin E and one fish-oil capsule daily. These are necessary additions, I believe – helping to prevent blood platelets sticking together, I am told, and strengthening the heart.

[It may be good to insert here that G.W.'s family did not agree that it was a good idea to reduce his C.V. tablets and hastily put him back on to a full dose on his return to England!]

Mon. 11-3-96. Rose at 4 a.m. Reflected on yesterday and the mistake I made, saying that 'There was no blood in the book of Revelation,' when I should have said, 'no blood in New Jerusalem.' Is that mistake an indication of my failing memory, and a suggestion that I should withdraw from preaching? If so I shall do so with reluctance and sadness. I shall be guided by the Lord. I know my natural powers are failing, but preaching has been part of my life for so long now, that to live apart from it is a saddening thought to me.

Tues. 12-3-96. Yesterday was spent amicably. I went to sleep in the afternoon. I feel the effects of preaching much more than I used to, but God grants grace and I love to preach. I believe that the Lord has sustained me for this purpose and I mean to do so as long as he enables me.

BACK TO ENGLAND.- A YEAR IN YORKSHIRE

So, with renewed resolve, as well as renewed energy from his prolonged break in Sydney, G.W. returned to Bracknell and his daughter's care. The care was not constant, though, as her father's ministry, though vastly curtailed, continued around the U.K.. Many fellowships, though realising that G.W.'s speaking engagements now had to be limited, still valued his visits to them, and felt that the power of God was still with him in a marked way.

One of the things he loved to do regularly was teach at the Christian

Workers' Programme in Birmingham, where he lectured on Bible topics, as previously described. The students loved to listen to him. Several times over the years it had been suggested to GW. that he ought to be training young people for the ministry. Various ideas for Bible colleges were discussed, but none of them materialised and G.W. did express regrets about this in later life. His efforts in this direction were confined mainly to week or weekend-long 'Bible Schools', some lectures abroad and the C.W.P. The great love of his life was for preaching and Bible exposition and these remained his forte.

Once, when in his eighties, GW. was visited by one of his colleagues, who had first met him when he had come to speak at the Birmingham Bible Institute. He asked him this question:

'Do I remember correctly? Did you say, when you came to B.B.I. that, when you were young and in the timber business, you were able to reconstruct the New Testament from memory?'

'It wouldn't be word perfect,' came the reply, 'but I knew what came in every next verse: I couldn't do it now, but I could do it then.' The colleague commented,

'When somebody knows the Bible like that, he is safe to give revelation to. When all a man's thinking is shaped; when his mind-set is Biblical, new revelations can be added that the Church doesn't have, and they are utterly consistent with what the Bible says.'

Though all was well whilst G.W. was able to carry on with his limited itinerary, life could be quite difficult for him and the family, especially during the winter months, when Dad had to stay at home because of recurring chest infections. The trouble was that he was only truly happy when he was able to preach. Though he preached at the Bracknell church on Sundays, when at home, and occasionally at some other nearby fellowships, he was restless and felt useless when not able to do what he had lived for all his life. He had hoped to die preaching; but this was not to be.

This is not to say that G.W. was a difficult person to please. He was always expressing gratitude for what was done for him and sometimes said that he hoped he wasn't a burden. Daughter, Judith, when telling a colleague at work that her father was living with her, was asked whether he was cantankerous.

'Oh, no,' came the reply. 'He's always good-tempered and saying how grateful he is.' This made her realise that perhaps other people had to suffer more than she did. However, when the owner of their house expressed a wish to sell it, offering a newly refurbished home, further out into the countryside, G.W. was pleased by the idea. The owner did stress, however, that G.W. could stay in his present home for as long as he wanted. The new home was set, together with the owner's own house and business premises, in a large acreage of grounds. This would be ideal for G.W.'s daily constitutional.

Moreover, he was interested in being cared for, for a while, by some old friends, John and Gwen Norris, with whom he had worked at The Longcroft in the 1960s and on many occasions since. The two families had become close over the years and John and Gwen had sometimes expressed a desire to help look after G.W. in his old age. John and Gwen were contemplating a move to Bracknell, after leaving their fellowship in Warrington and, for church and family reasons, G.W.'s family did not want to move out of the town. So new living arrangements were put into place, to everyone's satisfaction, the family still helping with their father's care.

However, during this period, it became clear that looking after G.W. was becoming a more continuous job. What to do about living arrangements for him was a problem. He had no home of his own, and neither of his daughters living in Britain owned a house large enough to cater for his needs.

A solution to the problem came about when youngest daughter Carole was asked by good friends, Peter and Rhoda Hitchen, whether she would like to take her father to live with them in their new B.+B business venture in the Yorkshire Dales. She could help them in setting up and working in the B+B, and they would all look after her father. He was pleased by the prospect of living in the Dales, and he loved Peter and Rhoda, who had been most kind and generous to him in recent years. He had stayed with them many times.

In the meantime his brother-in-law, Alf had passed away and G.W.'s nieces suggested that he should visit Australia one more time to stay with his older sister. They felt that he and Rene would be company for one another, both now having lost their spouses. This G.W. resolved to do, but this time the family insisted that he should travel Business Class, considering his advanced age and the length of the journey. After

An Ageing Preacher

some weeks with his sister, G.W. travelled to Malawi to visit his daughter Marian and her husband. Whilst there, he was pleased to be able to do some teaching to the pastors of the local churches.

On the return journey, he was singled out by the flight crew as being the oldest passenger on board and was presented with two bottles of Champagne by the captain. The family were greatly amused to see their father, looking rather ashamed, clutching the bottles and asking whether they could be used for cooking!

Whilst he had been away, his daughter Carole had gone up to Bell Busk, in the Dales, to begin working at the B+B. So, on his return in 2000, G.W. began a period of about twelve months in Yorkshire.. During this time he enjoyed daily walks in the picturesque countryside around Tudor House, as his new home was called.

He also greatly enjoyed being able to speak at regular Sunday afternoon meetings in the large comfortable lounge of the house. These have been described as 'wonderful meetings'. A ladies' weekend and a Whitsuntide weekend were held. At the Whitsun weekend G.W., who had taken to sitting down to preach, surprised everyone by standing up to speak because he felt, unusually now, that he had the strength to do so. The sermon given then was described as 'a wonderful, wonderful message ' by one who remembered it.

When it began to be difficult to run meetings in the house because of the numbers attending, a hall up the road was hired for the purpose. Also some small meetings were held in the house of some friends in the neighbourhood. One such meeting there was described as, 'The best meeting I have ever been in in my life.' So, although failing in many ways, G.W. still carried the powerful presence of God with him.

Leeds Fellowship was another place at which G.W. ministered during these last days in the UK. But, towards the end of this period at Tudor House Carole had to tell him that he had begun to repeat himself in meetings.

'Please tell me if ever I do that,' had been his request; but,

'I'll never forget the look on his face when I told him,' was his daughter's recollection. 'It was the hardest thing I have ever had to do,' she said. She did feel, however, that this time in Yorkshire had been a very happy time in her father's life and that his ministry there to small groups was 'very powerful'.

Many people visited him there, including his old friends and colleagues, Norman and Jenny Meeten. Another welcome visitor with his wife Hazel was Bernard Hull, with whom he had shared conference platforms. G.W. was convinced that God had healed him some years previously through Bernard's prayers. At the time he was being investigated for throat cancer and had been moved by the fact that Bernard had wept as he had been praying for his older colleague. It was the love in that prayer that he believed had saved him.

And, as well as by the love of old friends, his heart was warmed by the kindness he experienced at Tudor House, where he was royally looked after. However, as their father was now becoming very forgetful, it was felt by the family that he should now be cared for solely by them. This may have seemed like the end of his ministry, but it was not to be so.

CHAPTER 9
A PREACHER PROMOTED

MALAWI

G.W.'s daughter Marian and her husband Martin had been forced to leave their work in Zimbabwe and were now doing missionary work in Malawi, near Blantyre. They had been extending their rented house, partly in anticipation of having their father to live with them. Now the family, including Dad, felt that the time had come to take him away from any sense of duty or responsibility in Britain, letting him end his days as he had expressed a wish to do, in Africa.

He loved the warm weather, and it was becoming impossible for anyone to stay in the same room with him in England, the heating would have to be turned up so high! The spacious house in Malawi was on one level, the extensive grounds being ideal for the daily walks which G.W. insisted on taking right up until the final weeks of his life.

So, after spending four months with his eldest daughter in Bracknell, during which time he had been able to attend his youngest grandchild's wedding and spend some time with his two great grand children, he left Britain in 2001 for the last time. Before he left, many old friends, who, no doubt, realising that they would probably never see him again in this world, came to visit him to say goodbye. Knowing that he would not be buried alongside his wife, he bequeathed his grave to his eldest daughter.

'You can have it, Judith!' were his generous words.

'Thanks very much, Dad!'

For his first six months in Malawi, G.W. was in good health and enjoyed being able to be useful once more. Beside growing things in the garden, he was delighted to be asked to minister to the local pastors and their wives, who came to the house for various meetings and conferences.

They relished the chance to listen to his teaching. Amos, the Muslim house boy, interpreted G.W.'s messages to the ladies' meetings, as well as helping to care for the ageing preacher. Old age is very much respected in Malawi and he was known as 'Agogo', a term meaning Grandfather in the local language.

As well as relishing the lovely fresh fruit and vegetables from the garden, G.W. thrived on the social life he enjoyed when Marian took him round visiting her friends, including those from the school at which she taught. He loved being able to sit outside for much of the day, being away from the British climate. Family and friends were able to visit him in the spacious house and, to his joy, his daughter Carole spent many months there, helping with her father's care.

When his health began to deteriorate Marian was able to hire Mavis, a Christian nurse from the Seventh Day hospital in Blantyre. Mavis looked after her father for one day a week, so that she could go out. After Amos had left Marian's service the new house-keeper, Eveline, a lovely Christian lady, also put herself out to care for 'Agogo'. All this attention was greatly appreciated by the recipient and helped to keep him cheerful.

Moreover, one of the dogs became especially attached to the now 89 year old man and took to sitting by his chair for hours on end. G.W. had always liked animals; but the family had never owned pets, perhaps because Dolly had never wanted them. Now he could enjoy the company of the dogs, kept mainly for security.

There were always plenty of visitors to the house, including teams of young people and others, come to help with the work. Besides this, the family were able to take their father for a couple of short holidays; one to Lake Malawi and another to a more local beauty spot in a mountainous region near Zomba. So his life was eventful and interesting, probably much more so than it could have been had he remained in England. The warmth of the Malawian people, as well as the warmth of the sun, was a great comfort to him. Malawi is known as 'the warm heart of Africa', and he proved this to be true.

During the last six months of his life old friends, Fran and Terry Watson, looked after their 'Father in the Faith,' as they considered him, for three weeks, whilst the family were on leave. They said that they were 'thrilled to have had the opportunity of being with him during the last few months in this life,' and that 'during times of reading and prayer at the end of the day his heart was truly in fellowship with God,' though he had weakened. A little later Norman and Jenny Meeten were welcome visitors, but whilst they were there G.W. had to be taken into hospital; his health was giving concern. They returned to England knowing that he was not long for this world.

Now G.W. was approaching his 90th Birthday and his eldest daughter and her husband, with their son, were due to visit their father to help celebrate the occasion. They collected up cards and presents from all the family, wondering whether he would ever receive them.

They arrived to find that Dad, having had a spell in a Blantyre hospital, was now installed in the hospital wing of Newlands, a complex of houses and nursing home run by German Catholic Sisters for retired expats. It was, the family felt, an answer to their need that their father had been given a place there, though he had not been in the country for long enough to qualify for this privilege. Newlands was near to their home and the quality of care from the dedicated Sisters was outstanding. It seemed to be God's provision for them all and the very best alternative to care at home which would now have been impossible.

90th birthday cards were flooding in and they were all read and shown to the patient before being used to adorn the room. As well as congratulations on his 90 years, the constant theme of the cards, repeated again and again, was one of gratitude to God for ever having known G.W., testifying to the fact that he was a 'Father in the Faith' to so many people. They thanked him for his 'love and care over the years' and for his 'wonderful example' and the ministry that had 'changed' their lives.

The affection that poured out of the cards must have comforted him in his last days. Words such as 'eternally grateful to God for you' and 'without you we would never have come to know the Lord in such fullness' must have filled his heart with joy, though he could not say much. Several people quoted from St' Paul – *I thank my God upon every remembrance of you.*

On their father's 90th birthday, 27th April 2003, his daughters and their husbands, with a few friends and the nursing Sisters celebrated with cake and fizz [non-alcoholic!] in the hospital room, decorated for the occasion. How much the nonagenarian appreciated his 'party' was in question; but it was quite a jolly gathering, nevertheless.

The celebrations over, the family began to be concerned that their father might linger on in distress for many days, unable to move around or do anything for himself. Two days after the birthday, whilst visiting their father, the doctor had told them that she was not expecting him to die for some time because his heart was so strong. Some friends had kindly offered to make a meal for them. During the meal they all joined hands and prayed that the Lord would end their father's suffering and take him home.

No sooner had they returned to their own house after the meal than a call came from Newlands for them to hurry to the hospital, where they found that the patient had already passed peacefully away. The Sister who was with him told them,

'This was a holy man.'

Whether, had he had the choice, G.W. would have chosen to be cared for in a room with a crucifix on the wall outside the door is doubtful. But there is no question that his care was lovingly given and that his last days were a testimony to his Lord, as he would have wished.

FUNERAL

The place chosen for the funeral was Thyolo Road Cemetery, close to his daughter's home. It was held on a Sunday. Unaware of the situation, Derrick Harrison, an old friend and fellow leader, was visiting Malawi on a stop-over from Kenya. The family were thankful that he was there and able to play the accordion for the funeral, which was held around a shelter in the centre of the cemetery.

Vincent Chirwa, a local minister from Blantyre Baptist Church, which the family sometimes attended, took the service and preached. It was a very simple occasion with a congregation of thirty Malawian pastors and wives and about twenty other local friends joining the family. John Valentine had flown in from Zimbabwe to attend the funeral and he spoke at the graveside of how the Gospel had been spread in parts of Africa 'through this man,' as he put it. John's wife, Celia, wrote in her weekly Ameva report that:

'The work of Ameva would not have happened without the life and ministry of G.W. North. He has many children, grandchildren and great grandchildren in the Faith in Africa, and indeed all over the world. The ripples of a life given to God are truly infinite and eternal. We believe that he was one of the greatest Bible expositors of his generation. His legacy is 'Fruit unto God' [the title of one of G.W.'s books].

Included in the congregation were two graduates of Ameva Bible College, Zimbabwe, who had heard G.W.'s lectures there. One of them had travelled 300k, a great distance in his terms, to bring his condolences. As is the custom in Malawi, family and friends stood at the graveside whilst it was being back-filled. All the while a choir, consisting of the pastors and their wives sang Chichewa choruses. Several hymns in English were also sung. It was an unforgettable sight and sound on that beautiful Malawian hillside. G.W. would have loved the drama of it all!

And he would have loved the fact that all the pastors and wives were afterwards included in a meal at the Blantyre Club; something which would have been a rare experience for them, and paid for by him, with almost the last money from his bank account. As Celia said in her report:

'Mr. North said that he entered the world with nothing and it was his intention to leave it with nothing.' How pleased he would have been to see the people gathered there!

After the burial Pastor Chirwa had shown the family the grave where he had buried his young wife only weeks earlier, reminding them that a man who had lived until the age of 90 was a rare thing in that country. It was a humbling thought that this pastor, who had just conducted the funeral for them, had visited them and expressed his loving concern for them. How gracious he was! They felt honoured to be standing there with such a servant of God.

One of Marian's work colleagues commented that her father's funeral had been 'a good funeral, markedly different from many others that are full of crying and wailing, as seem common in this country. We only knew him as Agogo, and I remember him as a very happy person. He will continue to be a happy person in God's presence.' The family's aim in taking their father away from the pressures of living in England had been fulfilled and his last two years were relatively untroubled.

Six months later a memorial service was held in Bracknell. Hundreds of people, from home and overseas gathered to remember the man whom many regarded as their spiritual 'father'. It was a wonderful occasion, full of praises to God.

LOOKING BACK

At this memorial service Fred Tomlinson, a Fellowship leader from Canada, who had been a young man when he first met G.W. in the early Liverpool days, was distributing a booklet he had written, called, 'Many learn the words, few the song', a quotation which G.W. himself had used. The booklet contains 'personal memories of Mr. G.W. North, a truly remarkable man,' and states the writer's belief that whilst 'other ministering brethren were also becoming prominent, this man was uniquely prepared by the Lord to carry an essential message for that period in time'.

The time he refers to was the early 1960s, which, he says, 'was a time of turmoil and unrest in the UK. Young and old alike were desperately searching for reality and meaning in life. Several issues combined to create this crisis. These included the sexual revolution and the use of illicit drugs; but by far the most serious factor was that Christianity had degenerated into a severely weakened state, having virtually lost its prophetic voice.' The writer quotes from the book of Esther, saying that G.W. was a man sent *for such a time as this.* Numerous men in leadership positions in many countries can trace their spiritual roots to the ministry of Mr. North.'

A more personal memory of the preacher from Fred was that he 'was always impressed with Mr. North's personal conviction.'

'In the early days,' he says, 'when we first met him, not only did his radical preaching catch our hearts' attention, but his strong convictions and Christ-like life captured our imaginations. Although he was some thirty years senior to us, we never thought of him as old; he made ageing seem attractive!'

On the down side, he has to admit that, 'The black and white, radical, sometimes blunt manner of Mr. North didn't please everyone. There were those who misunderstood him, misrepresented him and disliked him. But one thing is indisputable; he leaves behind a wonderful legacy – the legacy of an elevated and clarified benchmark of the Christian life.'

Beside this, of course, the family received many messages of condolence after their father's death which gave a good indication to them of the regard in which their father had been held by so many people. The messages spoke of his 'immense output to so many thousands,' of his 'dedication, diligence and faithfulness', and of his being 'fearless to declare what God had given him, yet at the same time radiating the love of God'.

'We owe so much to him,' one letter confessed, 'because he brought us, through love and nurturing, into the life of God which he knew for himself.'

One missionary to Brazil said that she could never have returned there to carry on her work, 'except for the Lord's touch', through G.W. 'He was God's very special prophet and lovely man to all of us,' she said.

One family wrote that he 'touched our lives with a profoundness unmatched by any other living man.' 'He has left much influence,' wrote another. - 'I cannot help but think of him with a smile on my face as I owed him so much,' was another one's testimony.

'Along with countless others, I bless the Lord for the day G.W.N. was born,' one person said, and spoke of 'so many thousands' being brought into a 'spiritual heritage' through him.

A letter from Canada stated that G.W. was known as 'The Apostle of love. He so presented the Lord and His Gospel to us that anything seemed possible. We were always challenged by his life and preaching to come up higher.'

Another couple stated that, 'He would never have wanted an accolade, and that 'his very presence was both a wonderful blessing and a challenge; yet with this challenge came also encouragement and support.'

One person said that he rejoiced 'at the spiritual insight and preciseness' of G.W.'s interpretation of the Scriptures', and stated that he hadn't heard better.

A missionary in Sudan wrote – 'The fruit is incalculable. I am just one of thousands snatched from Hell by his teaching and ministry.'

A couple wrote from Chegutu, Zimbabwe, - 'At church I said I wanted to give the congregation a bit of advice from Mr. North. I said I was going to give them Mr. North's plan for victory in their lives. He told me to read St. John's Gospel twenty times and then when I had finished, to read St.

John's Epistles twenty times.' They had picked up on something which G.W. had urged people to do many times throughout his preaching career. John's Gospel was his favourite source of ministry; but whenever he preached he would urge people to read the Book for themselves; not just to take things from him. They needed to immerse themselves in The Scriptures, as he had done.

'You read it when you get home!' was his constant cry.

'He brought a touch of Heaven into our lives,' remembered one couple, who talked of the 'Christ like' way he had ministered to them. Another person called him 'Your gentle father,' and wrote of his 'unwavering example of obedience to Jesus, whatever the personal cost.'

G.W.'s niece Lorna wrote from Australia. Her two sisters had travelled over from Sydney to speak at his memorial service; but she could not come:-

'Uncle Wally set a standard which he never compromised and from which he never deviated. The standard was high, commensurate with his sense of calling, and he called us to settle for nothing less than God's best, but always to *press on toward the mark*. He had a consuming passion for Jesus and a burning desire to introduce people to the God who is LOVE. He had a beautiful voice and a deep love of music; a sweet memory is of him singing, "Beloved, let us love"[a hymn by Horatius Bonar c. 1880]. This was his heart, and the driving force which defined his life and teaching.'

One correspondent sent in an account for this biography of his first encounter with G.W. back in 1984 in Bradford. He reported:

'I heard several speak of him in glowing terms, and I wondered if some were going beyond healthy appreciation and were setting him on a pedestal. He was booked in for a mid-week meeting in our church – and, to be honest, I had started to react a little against the highly complimentary comments that some were making. I wondered if I would sense his ministry as being special.

I can so clearly remember the opening few minutes of his talk. He commented on the opening text of Romans-" *Paul, an Apostle*. He didn't have to try and be an apostle – He was one. You become with ease what God says you are. Don't try to be something."

It was as though a light switched on in my mind and I was hooked.

I marvelled that Mr. North was drawing simple things from the text that came across so powerfully. I also remember the great authority and apparent effortlessness that characterised his ministry. I try to follow his example when I preach.'

A Fellowship leader in Canada wrote about his 'Dear Chinese students of whom 'one and another had realised quite spontaneously what it meant to be free from sin and to have a new heart. I'm sure that the work God is doing amongst these students is part of the out flow of the river that flowed through Mr. North. There must be thousands of other people all over the world to whom and through whom that same river is flowing.'

Another present day leader and conference speaker says of G.W. 'That man had mastered that Book. He knew every part of it. It was at his fingertips. He didn't need a list of verses when he was preaching. The fire touched that.

One of the things that excited me was the way he expounded Salvation in terms of the New Covenant. He was really asking the question, "Are you in the New Covenant?" The elements of the New Covenant are that *I will give them one heart, and I will put a new Spirit within them and take the stony heart out of their flesh and give them a heart of flesh.* [Ezekiel, 11]. What he was saying was that "If this hasn't happened you're not in the New Covenant." This is really strong stuff. This is radical. This kind of thing for me was what opened my heart to the man. It has to be entire and fully functioning or it doesn't work. There's something about an apostle which makes him very creative. There was something about that man. He wasn't just a gifted pastor; he wasn't just a gifted preacher; he wasn't just a gifted evangelist; he wasn't just a gifted teacher; he was a man uniquely chosen for his generation.'

The words quoted here are typical of the claims that G.W. was 'a man raised up by God', to affect many lives in his generation. When asked, for this biography, how wide an influence he thought G.W. had had, Norman Meeten pointed the author to some talks he, Norman, had given at The Longcroft on the origins and spread of the Fellowships up until 2008. He was describing how the leaves which he had seen in Liverpool, blown by the wind of the Spirit, had, in fact, settled in many, many places all over the world. The preacher, fresh from the fire which had burned in Bradford, had played his part in kindling this fire in the hearts of those he taught in Liverpool.

In the Longcroft talks Norman used another metaphor, speaking of 'this remarkable tapestry, connecting this person and that person, with no human manipulation.' Besides Fellowship links in this country, he cited individuals and groups in sixty six countries with which those Fellowships had direct contact. These have sprung up, without any efforts to expand, directly or indirectly, from those early Liverpool days, some of them being in countries where there is no religious freedom and others in countries in which Norman has preached over the years and visits regularly.

DIFFERENT VIEWPOINTS

Writers unconnected with GW. perhaps provide a more balanced, though not up to date view of the significance of the Fellowships associated with him[sometimes dubbed 'The North Circular'].

Andrew Walker's 'Restoring The Kingdom'[1989] states that 'Whilst his fellowships have their roots before the Charismatic Renewal Movement, Pastor North is a truly charismatic figure in the way in which his character and doctrines are treated as out of the ordinary by his followers. His fellowships are throwbacks to the Holiness movements of the nineteenth century and the perfectionist teachings of John Wesley.' He also recognises that G.W. North pursued a full-time itinerant ministry 'with considerable success.'

Walker goes on to say that, 'Pastor North has always insisted that he is not the founder of a denomination, but it would not be unfair to say that all the fellowships that he has encouraged or overseen bear the imprint of his personality and teachings. His doctrines, by Evangelical and Pentecostal standards, contain elements of heresy. For instance, to be 'born again' is not, for North, the 'being saved', of Evangelicalism or the forgiveness of sins. New Birth is to enter the fullness of the Holy Spirit.'

Walker was of the opinion that 'this not only means the collapse of the 'second blessing' of Pentecostalism to one experience of spiritual initiation, it also implies a 'walking in the Spirit' that is synonymous with sinlessness' and gives this as the reason for his opinion that 'the North approach would never become a recipe for large organisations,' in this rather condemnatory perception of G.W.s teachings.[It has been protested that this is a misrepresentation of G.W.'s teaching by someone who did not know him].

He continues by giving his view that, 'It is difficult to envisage the perfectionist teaching of Pastor North having much success without his personal charisma. He has expressed the view himself that the vision dies with the man.'

The Catholic writer, Peter Hocken, in 'Streams of Renewal', calls GW. North a 'prominent figure in one of the strands of the House Church movement' and talks of his links with significant leaders of the Renewal movement. But he also observes that his 'network of influence was less central to the evolution of the Charismatic Movement than the Fountain Trust and other streams' examined in his study.

On G.W.'s teaching, Hocken writes, 'His concern not to separate the Spirit from the person of Jesus has been a central thrust in the teaching of G.W. North.....Although aspects of North's teaching are questionable, there is something about his main thrust that is truly faithful to the New Testament, as, for example, *At that day [Pentecost], you shall know that I am in my Father and you in me and I in you.* [John 14]. This was the dearest wish in Jesus' heart for them; it is by far the most important thing that takes place in the Baptism in/of/with the Holy Spirit.'"

Joyce Thurman in 'New Wineskins'[1982], after interviewing G.W. for her thesis, reported that, 'Mr. North himself realises that he will be accused of heresy; that is the price of claiming an absolute truth that others have missed. He states there was a great need for reformation of Christian doctrine, and sees the New Covenant of Christ starting at the day of Pentecost.'

In his M.A. Thesis, in which he examines G.W's writings, Derrick Harrison, a Birmingham Fellowship leader and founder of the Christian Worker's Programme, states that 'North found himself marginalised, though he was one of the first Charismatics to view Baptism in The Spirit in terms of conversion-initiation.'

A reason for this marginalisation, given by another fellowship elder is that,

'He [G.W.] actually said, "You're wrong! This is what's right!" Other people said, "This is what's right! This is what's right!" He was questioning people's experience. Most of the people who responded most deeply to G.W. were people who actually had a fully formed theology, but knew there were gaps in it. The present generation are left with a purity of doctrine and wonder what all the fuss was about.'

Another reason given for G.W.'s unpopularity in some circles is his focus on sin. 'The Charismatic Renewal did not see the Baptism in the Spirit as destructive of the old, to bring in the new. It did not have much to say about Holiness, which was a central theme of G.W.'s preaching – *without which no man shall see the Lord* [Hebrews 12].'

The purpose of this biography is not to discuss theology; but it is worth quoting again from Fred Tomlinson's booklet:

'There was a sense in which he [G.W.] really did have just one message – the foundational message of the New Birth. The promise was of a radical transformation of life; a new heart, a new spirit and the indwelling Holy Spirit. The result would be a personal and powerful experience, which would plunge men and women into Christ's death, while, in the same moment, flooding them with His holy life. Mr.North knew that any attempt to construct a Christian life without this function would be inviting frustration and failure. Little wonder that he said if he were a local pastor again he would preach the New Birth message at least once every month.'

To finish on a more personal note, and one which G.W. himself would probably have liked to hear, from Mickey Wright of Scotland –

'I would say that in all my years as a Christian, I have never met anyone quite like Mr. North. He was a flesh and blood example in my generation of someone who was truly walking with God. The memory of him remains as an example to me, and sometimes, when I need encouragement, I say to myself –

"If Mr. North could live this life of faith, and he was just a man, then so can I!"

This is echoed by Roger Shuttleworth of London, Canada:

'I thank God for this man. He did more than teach me the Bible; he opened my eyes to spiritual reality as nobody else has done. He taught me the things of God, demonstrated them in his life and ministry, and convinced me that I could know Christ in the same way he did. God grant that we may see his like again!'

CONCLUSION

At his memorial service G.W.'s granddaughters sang one of his favourite hymns, which he used to sing as a solo. It sums up his life of love for his Lord.

Jesus, these eyes have never seen
That radiant form of Thine.
The veil of sense hangs dark between
Thy blessed face and mine.

I see Thee not; I hear Thee not.
Yet art Thou oft with me,
And earth has ne'er so dear a spot
As where I meet with Thee.

Like some bright dream that comes unsought
When slumbers o'er me roll,
Thine image ever fills my thought
And charms my ravished soul.

Yet, though I have not seen
And still must rest in faith alone,
I love Thee, dearest Lord, and will;
Unseen, but not unknown.

When death these mortal eyes shall seal
And still this throbbing heart
The rending veil shall Thee reveal,
All glorious, as Thou art.
          Ray Palmer[1858]

George Walter Govier-North began life being dedicated under the Salvation Army flag. The Salvation Army term for departed soldiers is 'Promoted to Glory!'

As one who has *fought a good fight*, so he is.

At his Malawi home with Benji

Afterword by Alan Raistrick

G IS FOR GRANDAD, TOO

My mother still laughs sometimes when I wear my "North Face" jacket, a reminder of the prodigious physical gift he gave to us both - the North Nose! I hope I wear it well.

Grandad has given me much more than this prominent feature, though, starting with my earliest memories of meeting any of my wider family when he and Nana visited us in Zambia in 1974 - the arrival of the kindly couple from England to see my newly born sister was definitely a special occasion.

Later childhood memories of Grandad are dominated by lots and lots of strangers. I distinctly remember the feeling of bewilderment amidst the bustling throngs at one of the house churches (I believe it was Belmont Road), often to be repeated; Grandad always seemed to be in the middle of the crowds or in big rooms of people where children weren't allowed. It's not that I ever resented this, it's just the way it was - I guess some distance from family is inevitable for someone so sought after.

When he did get time, however, Grandad always had a smile, a hug and a playful ruffle of the hair - he'd always call me "boy", even when I reached my thirties! I remember very happy Christmases at Auchenheath House, sledging in the grounds and Christmas morning by the fire in Grandad and Nana's Lodge - a real postcard scene. Although at times he seemed almost other-worldly wise and extremely serious in his work for God, this was always balanced with humour, kindness and love for his family, especially the grandchildren.

This balance between man and preacher was powerfully illustrated much later, at Nana's death. Of course this was a very emotional time with many of her children and grandchildren in the hospital room during her final hours, understandably upset, but I clearly remember Grandad at her bedside, calm and in control, praying continually and very obviously filled with assurance that she was shortly to be with God. This was a strong demonstration of his faith in its own right, but stronger memories come from the few moments I watched him when no one was looking to him for strength or expecting comforting words - for a few seconds, he was just a man losing his dear wife.

Sometimes it is contrast that brings most clarity, and this was true here for me – realising that this undisputed man of God was still just a man was the opening for me to begin to understand something of the core message of Grandad's work and, indeed, that this duality is in some ways the message itself. Thanks, Nana, for this.

A jumble of other memories criss-cross the events described elsewhere in this book, with some refreshed by reading it. One section in particular reminded me of a pointed comment from Grandad after I had given a reading at my younger sister's wedding. On observing my then customary all-black attire he asked "did you think you were coming to my funeral boy?" It's hard to see how my own career in video games and films could have been more different to his, but insights like these kept us talking. I am sure he would be happy that my wardrobe has since broadened to now occasionally include browns and denim.

Just as my memories of Grandad began in Africa, so they ended 29 years later. His health had been deteriorating for some weeks, but to this day I still don't really know what made me decide to go to Malawi to see him on the spur of the moment. I had really not expected to see him again after he had left Yorkshire a year or so earlier and, even if I could get to him before he died, I had been told it was very unlikely he would recognize me, never mind be able to talk.

But go I did, and recognise me he did, and we were able to talk for a few moments – I believe it was the first time he had spoken in days. He gripped my arm with his still strong hand, pulled me close and said "it means a lot to me that you're here, boy". Nothing profound or especially inspirational, but this final connection between grandfather and grandson was all I needed to take with me and to this day it continues to help me understand what made him tick.

So, thanks Grandad – for the love, for the opportunity to know someone great at what they were put on this earth to do and for a bit of help with figuring out what life is about for myself – although I'm not there yet!